Possessions and Exorcisms

Fact or Fiction?

Other books in the Fact or Fiction? series:

Possessions and Exorcisms

Fact or Fiction?

Tom Head, *Book Editor*

Daniel Leone, *President*
Bonnie Szumski, *Publisher*
Scott Barbour, *Managing Editor*

OPPOSING
VIEWPOINTS®
SERIES

0 0022 0303107 1

GREENHAVEN
PRESS®

THOMSON
————*————™
GALE

Acknowledgments

Tom Head extends special thanks to project editor Kyla Stinnett, managing editor Scott Barbour, and production editors Lisa Mitchell and Andrea Nakaya. Charlie Brenner of the Jackson/Hinds Library System, Sherry Stroup of Kessler-Hancock Information Services, and Shane Hunt of 4ResearchSolutions.com all played an instrumental role in helping to locate hard-to-find research materials. As always, Tom would also like to thank his family for their love and support.

LIBRARY OF CONGRESS CATALOGING-IN-PUBLICATION DATA
Possessions and exorcisms / Tom Head, book editor.
p. cm. — (Fact or fiction?)
Includes bibliographical references and index.
ISBN 0-7377-1645-2 (lib. : alk. paper) — ISBN 0-7377-1646-0 (pbk. : alk. paper)
1. Demoniac possession. 2. Exorcism. I. Head, Tom. II. Fact or fiction?
(Greenhaven Press)
BF1555.P68   2004
133.4'26—dc21   2003048300

Printed in the United States of America

Contents

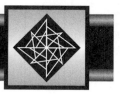

Foreword

"There are more things in heaven and earth, Horatio, than are dreamt of in your philosophy."
—William Shakespeare, *Hamlet*

"Extraordinary claims require extraordinary evidence."
—Carl Sagan, *The Demon-Haunted World*

Almost every one of us has experienced something that we thought seemed mysterious and unexplainable. For example, have you ever known that someone was going to call you just before the phone rang? Or perhaps you have had a dream about something that later came true. Some people think these occurrences are signs of the paranormal. Others explain them as merely coincidence.

As the examples above show, mysteries of the paranormal ("beyond the normal") are common. For example, most towns have at least one place where inhabitants believe ghosts live. People report seeing strange lights in the sky that they believe are the spaceships of visitors from other planets. And scientists have been working for decades to discover the truth about sightings of mysterious creatures like Bigfoot and the Loch Ness monster.

There are also mysteries of magic and miracles. The two often share a connection. Many forms of magical belief are tied to religious belief. For example, many of the rituals and beliefs of the voodoo religion are viewed by outsiders as magical practices. These include such things as the alleged Haitian voodoo practice of turning people into zombies (the walking dead).

There are mysteries of history—events and places that have been recorded in history but that we still have questions about today. For example, was the great King Arthur a real king or merely a legend? How, exactly, were the pyramids built? Historians continue to seek the answers to these questions.

Then, of course, there are mysteries of science. One such mystery is how humanity began. Although most scientists agree that it was through the long, slow process of evolution, not all scientists agree that indisputable proof has been found.

Subjects like these are fascinating, in part because we do not know the whole truth about them. They are mysteries. And they are controversial—people hold very strong and opposing views about them.

How we go about sifting through information on such topics is the subject of every book in the Greenhaven Press series Fact or Fiction? Each anthology includes articles that present the main ideas favoring and challenging a given topic. The editor collects such material from a variety of sources, including scientific research, eyewitness accounts, and government reports. In addition, a final chapter gives readers tools to analyze the articles they read. With these tools, readers can sift through the information presented in the articles by applying the methods of hypothetical reasoning. Examining these topics in this way adds a unique aspect to the Fact or Fiction? series. Hypothetical reasoning can be applied to any topic to allow a reader to become more analytical about the material he or she encounters. While such reasoning may not solve the mystery of who is right or who is wrong, it can help the reader separate valid from invalid evidence relating to all topics and can be especially helpful in analyzing material where people disagree.

Introduction

As a child growing up in 1930s New York, Jamsie Z. is followed around by a vision he calls Uncle Ponto. A shrill, foul-mouthed, and viciously cynical imp with blood-red eyes, Ponto is Jamsie's companion in rage against his criminal parents. When Jamsie becomes a radio broadcaster, Ponto is there to dictate fast-paced, edgy monologues that are a hit with listeners and guarantee Jamsie commercial success.

The story of Jamsie Z. and Uncle Ponto, described in Malachi Martin's *Hostage to the Devil: The Possession and Exorcism of Five Living Americans* (1976), starts off happily but grows gradually darker over time. As Jamsie begins to gain self-confidence and recognize his autonomy, Ponto goes on the attack, driving Jamsie's coworkers away, wrecking his social life, and tormenting him night and day with endless obscene rants, criticism, and—when all of that is not enough to break Jamsie's will—horrific visions. After considering suicide, Jamsie contacts a priest and finally undergoes an exorcism. Ponto is revealed to be a demon and, according to Martin, is driven out forever.

The story of Jamsie Z. is not unusual. Throughout history—and up to the present—accounts of demonic possession and exorcism have been told frequently. Today, many people continue to believe that human beings can be possessed by demons that must be exorcised. However, in recent years many observers—including most psychiatrists—have come to believe that people displaying behavior like Jamsie's are victims of severe mental illness, not demonic possession. The debate over whether possessions and exorcisms are fact or fiction often comes down to this religious belief in demons versus the scientific concept of mental illness.

Defining Possession and Exorcism

According to those who believe in the phenomenon, possession takes place when a person's mind is infested or taken over by a nonphysical being, usually an evil or tormented one. Most documented cases of possession involve victims who believe themselves to be possessed, but most religious traditions also hold that it is possible to be possessed without knowing it. Dramatic, supernatural effects—such as levitation, superhuman strength, physical transformation, and uncanny knowledge of foreign languages or other esoteric subjects—have been associated with possession, though many consider these phenomena to be extremely rare. The possessed sometimes report that they can see and hear demonic beings that are often horrific beyond description or, at the very least, annoying and disconcerting. Possession can also have a seductive component, as victims frequently claim that the infesting spirit encourages or forces them to engage in acts that violate their beliefs.

Religious traditions sometimes differ in their explanations of why possession happens. According to some religious thinkers, tormented spirits might invade human minds to avoid their own pain, as a sort of vacation from Hell. Rabbinic Judaism teaches that the spirit engaging in possession might not be evil but that its judgment may be clouded by extreme anguish and disorientation. Other traditions hold that evil spirits infest human minds solely because they enjoy causing pain and misery. However, the most common explanation—found in Islam and in most Christian exorcism traditions—is that evil spirits possess human beings in hopes of gaining a strategic advantage in their ancient war against love and justice. By provoking a victim to commit immoral acts, or simply by frightening the victim into submission, an evil spirit can convince an otherwise good person that he or she is a hopelessly corrupt lost cause—removing the victim's incentive to become a better person and increasing that person's chances of spending eternity in Hell.

For thousands of years religious leaders have attempted to drive away evil and tormented spirits using a ritual called exorcism, which attempts to rid people of demonic possession by calling on the power of the divine. Although some form of exorcism has existed in every major religious tradition (dating as far back as Babylonian mythology), the three traditions most relevant to mainstream American concepts of exorcism are those of the Abrahamic faiths: Judaism, Christianity, and Islam.

Exorcism in Judaism and Islam

In Judaism, possession is usually the work of a dybbuk rather than a demon. According to rabbinic tradition, a dybbuk is the wandering, tormented spirit of someone who died unhappy. The spirit either roams the earth in agony or seeks out a human host. Rather than casting the dybbuk into Hell, a rabbi's primary duty as exorcist is to relieve its pain. In the Midrash (rabbinic commentary) known as *Seder Eliahu Zuta*, the legendary Rabbi Akiba ben Joseph (ca. 50–ca. 132) comes across a dybbuk roaming the earth who can only enter Paradise if the son he has never met is taught how to pray properly, a skill that every Jewish child was expected to learn. Rabbi Akiba then dedicates a great deal of time to tracking down the boy and teaching him to pray and study the Torah, allowing the grateful dybbuk to leave his suffering existence and enter Paradise.

Although the belief in dybbuk possession has fallen away

in recent centuries, high-profile cases occasionally occur. In April 1999 Rabbi David Batzri is said to have cast out the dybbuk of a deceased Israeli man who had taken over the mind of his widow. The exorcism was broadcast on a number of independent radio stations, and a videotape was made of the event.

Islam, on the other hand, attributes the power of demonic possession to a race of evil spirits. In Islam, jinn ("the concealed") are invisible beings created by Allah (God) as a race of mortal creatures with free will, much like humans. The lord of the jinn is Iblis (Satan), an intensely evil being who has dedicated his existence to blaspheming Allah and punishing the human race. Some jinn have chosen to rebel against Iblis and ally themselves with Allah and the forces of good, but most follow Iblis on his path of sadism and destruction. Those jinn loyal to Iblis are referred to as *shaytans* ("adversaries"), and the Islamic tradition teaches that one of their powers is the ability to possess human beings. (Good jinn are prohibited from possessing human beings under all circumstances, as it is considered an intrinsically evil act.) Any Muslim can drive out *shaytans* by calling on Allah.

Exorcism in the Christian Church

Christianity draws its earliest traditions regarding possession and exorcism from the New Testament, which describes how Jesus Christ took on and established the role of Christian exorcist:

> When [Jesus] came . . . to the country of the Gadarenes, two demoniacs coming out of the tombs met him. They were so fierce that no one could pass that way. Suddenly they shouted, "What have you to do with us, Son of God? Have you come here to torment us before the time?" Now a large herd of swine was feeding at some distance from them. The demons begged him, "If you cast us out, send us into the

herd of swine." And he said to them, "Go!" So they came out and entered the swine; and suddenly, the whole herd rushed down the steep bank into the sea and perished in the water.[1]

Along with the ability to heal the sick, raise the dead, and cleanse lepers, the ability to cast out demons was attributed to Jesus' disciples. The first Christians brought this new ministry of exorcism into the church, where it would become an established rite used to cast out demons from the possessed. As the church expanded, the context of the rite changed. At the Fourth Council of Carthage (A.D. 255), exorcism became a required part of the baptism ritual for all non-Jewish converts. Most theologians of the time were concerned that a life lived outside of the context of Judeo-Christian tradition might have exposed the convert to demonic possession through unintentional demon worship. Another reason exorcisms were performed at baptisms was the concept of original sin, the belief that all human beings are already sinful at birth due to the original disobedience of Adam and Eve, which (according to traditional Christian theology) also brought death to the human race. As the doctrine of original sin became prevalent, exorcism gradually became a part of all baptisms—including infant baptisms. The exorcism performed as part of infant baptism (referred to as exsufflation) calls on the priest to breathe on the face of the infant three times, reciting, "Depart from him, thou unclean spirit, and give place to the Holy Spirit."[2] St. Augustine of Hippo (354–430)—remembered as the man who framed the doctrine of original sin as we know it today—defended the process of exsufflation by arguing that human beings are born into sin and death. "This," he writes, "is the reason why even little children undergo exsufflation, exorcism; to drive away the power of the devil their enemy, which deceived man that it might possess mankind."[3] When the

Christian Church experienced the Great Schism of 1054 and divided into two parts—the Roman Catholic Church and the Eastern Orthodox Church—both traditions continued to practice exorcism. Like the Roman Catholic Church, the Eastern Orthodox Church has included exorcism as part of the baptism ritual. The Greek Orthodox Church has also historically used exorcism to ward off a form of malignant envy called *vaskania* (the "evil eye"), which has often been regarded as demonic in character. Until the nineteenth century, exorcism rites were also represented in many Protestant traditions. The Church of England's original *Book of Common Prayer* (1549), for example, included an exorcism ritual that exhorted demons to "remember thy sentence, remember thy judgmente, remember the daye to be at hande, wherin thou shalt burne in fyre everlasting."[4]

Through the Great Schism, the Protestant Reformation of the sixteenth century, and the considerable reforms brought about by the Roman Catholic Counterreformation of the sixteenth and seventeenth centuries, the doctrines of demonic possession and exorcism have survived. The doctrine would face its greatest challenge at the hands of a relatively new scientific discipline called psychiatry, which usually dismisses exorcism as an outdated remedy for a nonexistent disease. According to most psychiatrists, demonic possession is nothing more than a symptom of mental illness.

A New Diagnosis

Prior to the eighteenth century, people exhibiting behaviors that today are viewed as symptoms of severe mental illness were commonly thought to be possessed. Over time, many came to believe that mental illness and demonic possession were two distinct problems that had to be dealt with in different ways. Mental illness was presumed to be a degrading and nearly always incurable condition. Little was known about its causes, and little could be done about it. Those who suffered from it were regarded in many respects as if they were dead, and were sometimes treated as if they were less than human.

During the late eighteenth century, a movement known as the Enlightenment encouraged scientific and secular thought over religious beliefs, which many Enlightenment thinkers had come to view as superstitious and backward. Mental illness was often regarded as a curable condition caused by imbalances in the body's humors, or natural fluids. For example, maniacal behavior might be caused by an excess of blood or an insufficient amount of black bile, and depression could be caused by an insufficient amount of blood or an excess of black bile.

By the early twentieth century, psychiatrists such as Sigmund Freud (1856–1939) had established new, highly sophisticated behavioral theories of mental illness that rendered the humors explanation obsolete and cast doubt on the reality of demonic possession. In his study titled *A Seventeenth-Century Demonological Neurosis* (1923), Freud discredited demonic possession by arguing that its symptoms could be more easily explained using the terminology of the new science called psychiatry.

Many psychiatrists since Freud have regarded symptoms that were attributed to demonic possession as signs of schizophrenia, a severe mental illness that can include hallucinations and identity disorientation. Other symptoms of schizophrenia include hearing voices that no one else hears and feeling that one is controlled by an outside force.

According to some psychiatrists, the symptoms of demonic possession can also signify multiple-personality disorder (MPD), a condition in which the victim unconsciously divides his or her personality into various alternate personalities. Joseph Mahoney, a mental health chaplain for the Roman Catholic Archdiocese of Detroit, has argued that some MPD symptoms may also resemble symptoms traditionally associated with demonic possession, including "the ability to cause in the observer a sense of cold, evil, or threat," "physical strength beyond ordinary perceptions of what is humanly possible," "hatred of God and religious objects," and "extreme self-mutilation."[5]

Some psychiatrists believe that different personalities may act independently of one another and that in some cases, one judging personality punishes the "guilty" personality for the victim's perceived transgressions. Psychiatrists generally treat people with MPD by helping them integrate their personalities and to learn to love and accept the "guilty" personality as part of their own identity. Many psychiatrists believe that by encouraging patients to demonize and reject aspects of their own personality, exorcism could make MPD symptoms worse.

By the 1960s psychiatry had driven the diagnosis of demonic possession underground. A few exorcists worked quietly in the background, but they generally did so with great discretion because exorcism was considered an embarrassing relic of medieval theology, completely alien to mainstream Western society. This was about to change.

The Return of Exorcism

William Peter Blatty's 1971 novel *The Exorcist* was an unlikely best-seller. Blatty, who had once been an aspiring priest, wrote the story of the possession and exorcism of an eleven-year-old girl, which he had loosely based on the actual diaries of an alleged 1949 exorcism. Both the book and the 1973 movie drew public attention to demons and the ancient rite used to expel them, and dozens of popular books followed. In the Blatty tradition, exorcists were regularly portrayed in movies and novels as fearless men who stared down the most powerful evil forces in the universe armed only with their faith and determination. Suddenly, being a known exorcist carried less stigma—and people who believed that they might be possessed by demons could find people willing to confirm their suspicions. "William Peter Blatty had obviously started something," sociologist Michael W. Cuneo writes in *American Exorcism: Expelling Demons in the Land of Plenty* (2001), but "it's unlikely even he knew exactly what it was."[6]

In 1999 the Roman Catholic Church revised its Rite of Exorcism for the first time in 380 years. This decision was made in response to a vast increase in the number of exorcists and an increasing demand for their services. Until the 1990s relatively few exorcists (probably no more than a few dozen) practiced in the United States and Europe. Today, there are at least three hundred. Gabriele Amorth, a Roman Catholic priest widely regarded as the church's senior exorcist, argues that public awareness of demonic possession has come at a particularly good time:

> Even if this battle against Satan concerns all men and all times, there is no doubt that Satan's power is felt more keenly in periods of history where the sinfulness of the community is more evident. For example, when I view the decadence of the Roman Empire, I can see the moral disintegration of that period in history. Now we are at the same level of decadence, partly as a result of the misuse of mass media . . . and partly because of Western consumerism and materialism, which have poisoned our society.[7]

As exorcism has become more popular within the Roman Catholic Church, it has also gained ground in Protestant churches of the Charismatic tradition. Charismatic theology teaches that good and evil forces fight invisibly for the souls of every human being and that demons are as active in the world as they have ever been—more active, perhaps, owing to the opulence and sensuality of Western culture. In an effort to fight demonic influence over human lives, Protestant ministers—and some Roman Catholic laypersons—perform a rite known as deliverance ministry, which is remarkably similar to exorcism but does not usually follow an established ritual. Whereas traditional exorcists read an established set of prayers, deliverance ministers are expected to rely directly on their faith and on the Holy Spirit to direct them as they proceed.

Because deliverance ministry does not operate within a strict organizational framework, its practitioners use extremely diverse methods. Some deliverance ministers restrain the possessed; others do not. Some believe that they must be physically present in order to perform the exorcism; others do so at a distance or even by telephone. Some involve the victim directly in the process; others dominate the victim in an effort to drive the demon away. The diversity of deliverance ministry means that no two deliverance ministers are likely to use exactly the same approach. However, all deliverance ministers do believe that demonic possession is a real phenomenon, not something that can be reduced to mental illness—though most also believe that mental illness should also be taken seriously and addressed appropriately by mental health professionals. Francis MacNutt, a former Roman Catholic priest who now serves as codirector of the nondenominational Christian Healing Ministries, regards deliverance ministry as an essential pastoral function that does not compete in any way with psychiatry:

> Ministers of the Gospel need to stop passing the buck by denying that demonic oppression exists or by simply referring people to psychiatrists or counselors when what is needed is deliverance. Counseling and medication may also be needed; and we should by all means cooperate with mental health professionals. But ministers must not continue to deny responsibility in their own field.[8]

How people interpret the recent surge of interest in demonic possession depends largely on how common they believe demonic possession to be. For those who believe that demonic possession never occurs or that it occurs only in extremely rare cases, demonic possession can easily appear to be just another pop culture fad. For those who believe that it is a serious, underestimated problem, this pop culture fad is a well-timed blessing.

Notes

1. *The Holy Bible (containing the Old and New Testaments with the Apocryphal/ Deuterocanonical Books).* New revised standard version. New York: Oxford University Press, 1989, Mt. 8:28–32.

2. Quoted in Peter Toon, "Exorcism," in *The New International Dictionary of the Christian Church.* Ed. J.D. Douglas. Rev. ed. Grand Rapids, MI: Zondervan, 1974, p. 365.

3. St. Augustine, "On the Creed: A Sermon to the Catechumens [De Symbolo ad Catechumenos]," trans. C.L. Cornish, in *A Select Library of the Nicene and Post-Nicene Fathers of the Christian Church.* Vol. 3. Ed. Philip Schaff. Grand Rapids, MI: Eerdman's, 1993, p. 369.

4. The Society of Archbishop Justus, "The 1549 Book of Common Prayer." http://justus.anglican.org.

5. Joseph Mahoney, "Exorcism and MPD from a Catholic Perspective." www.jmahoney.com.

6. Michael W. Cuneo, *American Exorcism: Expelling Demons in the Land of Plenty.* New York: Doubleday, 2001, p. 13.

7. Gabriele Amorth, *An Exorcist Tells His Story.* San Francisco: Ignatius, 1999, p. 29.

8. Francis MacNutt, *Deliverance from Evil Spirits: A Practical Manual.* Grand Rapids, MI: Chosen Books, 1995, p. 23.

Chapter 1

Fact or Fiction?

Evidence for Possessions and Exorcisms

Demonic Possession Is Real

Joe Beam

In recent years, there has been a growing movement within evangelical Christianity called *spiritual warfare*. The spiritual warfare movement teaches that God and his angels actively battle Satan and his demons for control of the world and for each individual human soul. Human beings can play a dramatic role in this struggle by living a holy life and battling moral decadence within their cultures.

Citing Biblical precedents, many theologians believe that demons can actively take over human lives. In this excerpt from his book *Seeing the Unseen* (2000), pastoral counselor Joe Beam makes a religious argument that demonic possession is a genuine threat.

As we prayed for her, she slipped from her chair and puddled on the floor. Her husband quickly moved to the floor with her and lifted her head into his lap, cradling her as he would one who was dying.

In a sense she was.

She moaned, cried out in pain repeatedly, and dripped tears enough to have washed the feet of Jesus. A clear phlegm-like substance seeped from her nose and her mouth, slowly covering her clothes. Sometimes her sobbed words were understandable. Sometimes they were so garbled that no one could make sense of them.

Sometimes other sounds coursed through the room that none present wanted to think about.

All the while, we continued to pray aloud. We called on the power of God. We asked Him specific things on her behalf. We repeatedly relied on the name of Jesus. So that she would not feel that we were trying to control her freedom or actions, we occasionally asked her if she wished us to stop, if she wanted us to leave.

No.

Whenever she said that word, it was always clear. She was in great pain, but she would not have us stop.

She wanted to be free.

I refuse to give any more details about what happened that day. . . . In just a few pages, I will tell you the result of our interaction, but first I want to give some very practical warnings about dealing with demons.

Demons Are Real, and Their Power Is to Be Respected

1. To Deny Demon Possession Is to Deny Scripture.

As a Bible-believing Christian, I must believe that people deny the inspiration of the New Testament when they explain away its demonic stories as misconceptions about diseases and the superstition of a simple people. While demons sometimes caused diseases or physical maladies, the demons were quite different from the malady itself. When Jesus spoke with the multitude of demons who called themselves Legion, they had identity, knew who He was, and begged Him not to cast them into the Abyss. Unless the New Testament writers fabricated the story, demons were real beings. Therefore, only those modernists who deny the inspiration of Scripture would deny that demons actually existed as real beings. The Scripture presents them as such, and all those who accept Scripture as the Holy Writ of God must accept them that way as well.

My guess is that nearly every Bible-believing Christian who read the above paragraph mentally gave it an amen.

But many Bible-believing Christians do deny the existence of demons today, using the same logic as those modernists who deny that they really existed in the New Testament era. The modernists say that in the New Testament, people who thought they had demons or met demons were simply superstitious and uneducated. Today many Christians say the same about those who truly believe they have encountered demons. These skeptics often justify their beliefs by citing a case where some overzealous Christian tried to cast out a demon when obviously the problem wasn't spiritual but emotional, psychological, or physical. They cry, "See! It's just superstition. Not demons! You guys need to accept the great strides in science and quit living in the darkness of religious fanaticism. Demon possession ended in the first century."

If you think that way, keep reading.

2. *Mistaken Diagnosis Doesn't Mean That Demons Don't Exist.*

It is undoubtedly true that many overzealous Christians—even ignorant and superstitious Christians—have claimed to have dealt with demons when no demons were present. What they encountered was nothing more than their own misunderstanding or misconception. Calling something a demon doesn't mean that it is. And it is undoubtedly true that some Christians have been badly hurt either emotionally, psychologically, or physically by those who assaulted them in an effort to remove the alleged demon. But that doesn't mean that demons don't exist.

Citing misdiagnosis and severe treatment of a supposed demoniac no more proves that demons aren't here than a jury's mistaken conviction of a murderer and his subsequent execution prove that there are no murderers. The occasional failure of our legal system doesn't mean that a jury cannot examine evidence and come to a logical conclusion as to the guilt of a defendant. In like manner, an occasional failure on the part of overzealous or misinformed Christians doesn't mean that none of us could ever correctly deduce that an individual is possessed by a demon or demonized.

Those who deny that spiritual warfare in our day includes the demonic typically relegate all human problems to the realm of the physician. Those who believe that spiritual warfare continues to involve the demonic all too often look for and find demons where none actually exists. Extremes on either side do not prove that either view should be discarded altogether.

When the true problem is physical or psychological, no one will cure the person by "casting out demons," because the problem isn't demonic. But at the same time, professionals who employ all that modern medical, pharmacological, and psychological science offers will continue to find that their methods will never heal some patients, because their problem isn't physical or psychological at its root. They aren't sick because of natural reasons, but because of supernatural reasons—specifically, demonic attack. People whose sickness is supernatural can be cured only by spiritual means.

3. Possession Is Rare and Must Be Proven!
It is common knowledge that the Catholic church has the most research and writings on the subject of demonology. While my own understanding of the Bible often puts me in conflict with Catholic views or doctrines, I find that some of their points hold great value to us who are non-Catholics. For example, though the Catholic church believes a person may be possessed by demons, they are likely the most skeptical group when it comes to believing that a specific individual is demon possessed. Because so many zealous people have attributed other human problems to the demonic, the Catholic tests to determine possession are quite extreme. In the General Rules Concerning Exorcism, they state:

> Especially, [the exorcist] should not believe too readily that a person is possessed by an evil spirit; but he ought to ascertain the signs by which a person possessed can be distinguished from one who is suffering from some illness, especially one of a psychological nature. Signs of possession may be the following: ability to speak with some facility in a strange tongue or to understand it when spoken by another; the faculty of divulging future and hidden events; display of powers which are beyond the subject's age and natural condition; and various other indications which, when taken together as a whole, build up the evidence.

Maybe we should be as careful in our assessment of demon possession ourselves. When the Holy Spirit describes cases of demon possession in the New Testament, they are extreme and unusual. That's why I said earlier that I've never encountered true possession.

But I have encountered the lesser level. . . . It isn't possession but demonization.

4. Gradual Awareness of a Lesser Level of Demonic Activity.
Catholics and Protestants alike are aware that while demonic possession is rare, there are other ways that demons operate. [Demonization] isn't possession and doesn't re-

quire an exorcism, as exorcisms are normally considered. But it does take Christians fighting the power of Satan by the power of the Holy Spirit.

5. Overcoming Demons Requires Preparation and Spiritual Authority. If that last paragraph makes you want to grab your Bible and go looking for a demon to deal with, slow down! Demons aren't weak, ineffective beings that any Christian can just saunter up to and order around. In dealing with demons, I recommend that we adopt the attitude expressed in Jude 9: "But even the archangel Michael, when he was disputing with the devil about the body of Moses, did not dare to bring a slanderous accusation against him, but said, 'The Lord rebuke you!'"

If the most powerful good angel we know anything about didn't confront Satan by his *own* power but instead said, "The Lord rebuke you!" we surely should maintain a respectful fear. Just because I know the name of Jesus and am a Christian doesn't mean that I am equipped to fight Satan's forces directly. In Ephesians 4, Paul makes it clear that becoming equipped requires training by those who are more mature. A couple of chapters later, in Ephesians 6, he tells us that facing evil requires armor and an offensive weapon. He goes on to let us know that when we are fighting spiritual war, we should involve intense prayer, even to the point of praying "in the Spirit" (6:18).

If you wish to fight the devil's forces (and I hope you grow to that point), you will have to operate under the authority of Jesus, or you yourself will be defeated as you attempt to free others. . . .

Confronting Demonization

A couple . . . came to me because they were convinced demonization existed in their home. Specifically, they believed the wife to be demonized. All types of experts, evaluations, and the like had indicated that her problem was neither mental, emotional, nor physical. With all those possibilities exhausted, they discerned that demons were present and asked my aid in overcoming them.

Discovering Footholds

Since I believe that a demonized Christian must have opened the door through some type of foothold, I interviewed her at length about any sin that she refused to quit or release. Based on my understanding of Ephesians 4:25–32, I specifically asked many questions designed to discover the existence of things such as:

• Lying
• Anger
• Stealing
• Slothfulness
• Unwholesome talk
• Bitterness
• Rage
• Brawling
• Slander
• Every form of malice
• Refusing to forgive

Carefully, I pointed out that if she were clinging to one of those evils, she gave the devil's forces a foothold within her. No matter how much we believed or prayed, until she "closed the breech" in her spiritual armor, the demons could come right back in. We read the scripture in which Jesus talked about how much worse the reinfestation is than the initial demonic presence (Matthew 12:43–45).

During the course of our conversation, I discovered that she held an intense hatred toward her stepfather who had repeatedly sexually molested her. She had never forgiven him and felt that she never could. The longer we talked, the more obvious it became to everyone in the room that her hatred and unforgiving spirit created the foothold that allowed her to be spiritually violated. That's how demons continually lured her into the same sin repeatedly. She felt helpless, out of control. I explained that by believing that she could not forgive her stepfather, she was believing a lie. She wasn't possessed but demonized. She was responsible for her actions and must take a firm stand against the devil's schemes. At the same time, we needed to separate her from her tormentors (demons) so she could have peace and time to heal.

Praying with Intense Faith

After a couple of hours of talking and studying, my "gentle instruction" led her to repentance. She finally understood that her lingering rage toward her stepfather caused him no punishment at all but was leading to her own spiritual failure. She forgave him, and then we all sought God in an intense prayer full of faith. She took responsibility for her own actions and admitted to herself that while she often felt out of control, she really did have control. She had been allowing her anger, hurt, and emotional confusion to so fog her mind that she repeatedly made sinful decisions. Now that she was in the process of forgiving her father and clearing her mind of her hurt and pain, she was beginning to remove the foothold. Now we needed to separate the evil beings from her just as surely as we would separate her from a lover who exercised undue influence over her. With her agreement and participation, we went to war through prayer.

During an hour or so of prayer, we did what Paul did and, in the name of Jesus Christ, commanded the demon to leave her.

I never asked its name. Never used my holy or sacred objects. Used no rituals or recitations. Did no binding by my own power or strength. (Like the archangel Michael, I called on the Lord to do the rebuking.) I and the minister who was there to assist called faithfully and regularly on the name of Jesus and in faith expected God to do all that had to be done to set the woman free.

He did.

She has been free for more than two years at the time of this writing and suffered absolutely no reoccurrence of the problems that led her to ask for help.

As directed, she went home and told her minister what had occurred and asked him to guide her in spiritual growth so that the demon could not return.

What If It Wasn't a Demon?

You may be thinking the same thing I felt for months after that encounter. What if the experts were wrong? What if the problem was emotional or psychological? Maybe all we did was offer her a form of positive suggestion instead of real deliverance?

Finally, I reached what I believe to be a sound and safe conclusion to the matter.

First, we did no harm.

- Neither the minister nor I tried in any way to convince her that she was demonized, thus causing further mental or emotional confusion on her part.
- We carefully considered the professional opinions of the medical doctors and psychologists who had examined her. We checked and double-checked to make sure that we did nothing contrary to their advice or opinion. While I don't rely on doctors to give me spiritual counsel or to make the final decision on spiritual matters, I do give great respect to their training and expertise.
- We did nothing to restrain her, unduly agitate her, scare her, or embarrass her. She had complete control of her

actions and freedom at all times.
- We did all we could to make her comfortable and safe.
Second, spiritual victory was won.
- Her problem had not been solved by the medical or psychological experts she had seen for years but was solved by confronting the demons she believed she had.
- Since we cannot see demons except on the radar of faith, we didn't look for an evil being to come snarling and tearing as proof that evil beings manipulated her. We believe that the *results* of the spiritual effort to remove demons proved its validity. Her problem was finally and completely solved.
- The woman and her husband have a wonderful marriage for the first time in twenty years.
- Her spiritual life is dramatically different now. She has a strong, faith-filled relationship with Jesus that is the guiding light to her life.

If you scoff because we saw no grotesque, drooling demon and cannot prove scientifically that he was ever there, I guess you'll scoff forever. I offer no other proof of our efficacy than the incontestable results in the woman's life. If I were to tell of things we saw, heard, smelled, and the like, I would only denigrate an act of spiritual war. Besides, since we have no examinable proof such as videos, you would have to take my word anyway.

And that, my friend, is an act of faith.

Why should you have faith in my veracity if you lack faith in the power of God to bring deliverance to one of His children?

Demonic Possession Can Cause Mental Illness

Roy Clements

Until the late nineteenth century, mental illness was often blamed on demonic possession. Although the idea of demonic possession is still deeply rooted in many faith traditions, it is generally seen as obsolete and superfluous from the perspective of contemporary psychiatry. The classic symptoms of demonic possession—malevolent inner voices, erratic behavior, and a tendency to think of oneself as irreparably evil—are symptoms of several common mental disorders.

Roy Clements, the author of the following selection, is an ordained Baptist minister with a Ph.D. in physical chemistry. He is currently on the staff of Imperial College, London. In this essay, which was intended for a conservative Christian audience with a high view of the Bible, he argues that the biblical model of demonic possession can still be

Roy Clements, "Demons and the Mind," *Cambridge Papers*, vol. 5, September 1996, pp. 1–4. Copyright © 1996 by Roy Clements. Reproduced by permission. www.royclements.co.uk.

meaningful to those suffering from mental illness. Rejecting what he calls the "dualistic" model that views mental illness and demonic possession as two separate phenomena, he favors a holistic model of mental health. According to this perspective, mental illness can be seen as resulting from any number of causes—including demonic possession. Clements affirms both the potential value of psychiatry in dealing with demonic possession and the potential value of religious rituals in dealing with mental illness.

The full text of this essay can be found on the author's website: www.royclements.co.uk.

From time immemorial societies have assigned supernaturalist interpretations to mental illness. Madness, it is held, is the result of the invasion of the human psyche by the spirit world. This invasion may be benign or even divine, as in oracular prophecy and mystic ecstasy. Alternatively, it may be malevolent, as in the case of witchcraft and demon-possession. The remedy in this latter case is exorcism.

This interpretation, however, has been opposed by two rival naturalistic explanations.

1. The organic model

On this view mental illness is the result of some physiological malfunction. Hippocrates in ancient Greece seems to have been the first to have regarded epilepsy as a physical illness due, according to his 'four humours' model, to an excess of 'phlegm'. This idea was preserved during the medieval period in the Arab world and re-entered Europe in the eleventh century as a result of the scholarly work of Constantine of Africa (c.1020–1087). With the growth of rationalism at the time of the Enlightenment and a more sophisticated understanding of the nervous system, the organic interpretation of mental illness gradually triumphed. The success of drug therapy in treating a variety of psychotic symptoms more recently has meant that this model now dominates psychiatric medicine.

2. *The psychodynamic model*

In 1923 Freud attempted a psychoanalytical interpretation of the case of Christoph Haitzman, a destitute seventeenth century artist who claimed he had become 'demoniacally possessed'. Freud argued that the 'demon' was in fact a 'personification of the repressed unconscious instinctual life' symbolising the subject's libidinal wishes towards his dead father. More recently, the post-Freudian school . . . has put the emphasis rather on early familial relationships. Haitzman's demon represents not so much repressed guilty impulses, as the internalised bad father himself.

Contemporary psychiatry, however, has not totally abandoned demonic terminology. A syndrome labelled 'possession' by [T.K.] Osterreich is still widely debated, though these days it is more usually termed 'multiple personality disorder' (MPD). The characteristic symptom is that the subject seems to be taken over by an alien 'alter ego'. Not all psychiatrists accept MPD as a diagnostic entity, but in the last forty years unprecedented numbers of such cases have been reported, particularly in North America. Claims that many of these are the result of the activities of clandestine satanic cults have led some psychiatrists to take the view that it may be therapeutically useful to collude with a patient's 'demonic' interpretation of their condition and look favourably upon a religious service of exorcism.

In general, however, most psychiatrists would regard the very idea of demon-possession as a relic of pre-scientific superstition. It is not really surprising, they would argue, that a severely disturbed person suffering from some kind of dissociative disorder finds it easy to rationalise their abnormal experiences in terms of assault by alien spirit forces, but such supernaturalist explanations are not to be seriously entertained.

Demon-Possession in the Bible

It is quite obvious, on the other hand, that Jesus and the apostles lived in a world that took for granted the existence of evil spirits and regularly ascribed mental illness to their malevolent activity.

Fear of demonic influences is notably less obvious in the Old Testament. Saul's insanity is ascribed to 'an evil spirit' (1 Samuel 18:10, 19:9), but significantly this is sent 'from the Lord'. And no mention is made of demons at all in respect of Nebuchadnezzar's psychotic breakdown (Daniel 4), though it had many of the characteristics of lycanthropy (the delusion of being a wild animal), a rare dissociative illness that is readily interpreted as 'possession'. It is strongly implied that the sinful pride of these kings was a major causative factor in their descent into madness. Daniel specifically advises Nebuchadnezzar to confess his sins if he wants to avoid this divine judgement.

Although illness is not always associated with some personal sin in the life of the sufferer (see Job), the Old Testament does indicate that such a link sometimes exists, either as a result of direct divine retribution (e.g. 2 Kings 5:27), or the self-destructive consequences of unresolved guilt (Psalm 32:3). No distinction is made between physical and mental illness in this regard. Those who are so afflicted are not treated as helpless victims, but as responsible sinners in need of repentance.

In the New Testament, however, the possibility of illness, and particularly mental illness, arising from assault by external evil forces is widely assumed. Demon-possession having the characteristics of MPD can be readily identified in the gospels. Notice, for instance, the plural inner consciousness in 'what have you to do with us?' (Mark 1:24) and 'my name is Legion; for we are many' (Mark 5:9). However, in the New Testament demon-possession is also attributed in many cases which do not fit the MPD pattern. In Mark 9:14–29 we read of a boy with 'a dumb spirit' who suffered from convulsions. This presumably implies that he was rendered mute by his affliction. That physical handicap like dumbness was sometimes ascribed to possession is clear from Matthew 9:32–33, 12:22, and Luke 13:11. Paul regards the oracular divination of a slave girl as due to an evil spirit (Acts 16:16). And the accusation that Jesus himself was possessed seems to be related to what his opponents interpreted as paranoid or megalomaniac delusions (John 7:20, 8:48, 10:20).

This does not mean that the New Testament writers had no access to any other vocabulary for describing madness. The word groups associated with *ekstasis* (Mark 3:21, 2 Corinthians 5:13) and *mania* (John 10:20, Acts 26:24, 1 Corinthians 14:23) are both used of being 'out of one's mind' though not necessarily in a malignant sense. And the verb *seleniazomai* (literally moon-struck, cf. English 'lunatic') may have been particularly associated with the distinctive symptoms of epilepsy (Matthew 17:15).

Two Different Phenomena?

Most Christians who have discussed the issue have sought to argue that the Bible uses this non-supernaturalist vocabulary to distinguish demon-possession from other forms of mental illness. This conventional viewpoint may be loosely designated as dualistic. It is attractive because it enables Christians to acknowledge the success of modern psychiatric medicine without totally abandoning the category of the demonic.

However, the biblical base for such a dichotomous interpretation of mental illness is thin. The text most frequently quoted in support of it is Matthew 4:24:

They brought to him all the sick, those afflicted with various diseases and pains, demoniacs [*daimonizomai*], epileptics [*seleniazomai*], and paralytics.

The evangelist, it is argued, is here distinguishing demon-possession from other forms of mental illness like epilepsy. But it is not at all clear that Matthew intends us to understand these words as mutually exclusive diagnoses. It is much more likely that this list is simply descriptive of certain kinds of observed symptom. As a result more than one term may sometimes apply to the same individual. We have in fact already noted several examples of such overlap. The epileptic (*seleniazomai*) boy is also demon-possessed in Matthew 17:14–21. Would the evangelist have wished to discriminate other epileptics who were not? On what basis would he have made such a distinction? Jesus is simultaneously accused of both mania and having a demon (John 10:20). Are there two different conditions or merely alternative descriptions of the same irrational state of mind? Equally, there are numerous examples in the gospels of physically handicapped individuals whose plight is not attributed to demons (e.g. the deaf-mute in Mark 7:31–37). Was there some observable difference in the mutes mentioned above (in Matthew 9 and 12) that led to them being regarded as demoniacs?

Diagnosing Possession

It is difficult to be confident about the answers to such questions. Jesus certainly employed a different technique when he healed those whose affliction was attributed to demons. He exorcised the evil spirits 'with a word' (Matthew 8:16–17), whereas in other healings he commonly used touch (e.g. Mark 7:33). Unusually, in the case of the crip-

pled woman (Luke 13:11–13) Jesus healed by touch, not exorcism, in spite of Luke's recorded diagnosis of 'a spirit of
infirmity'. Was this a case in which Jesus recognised the condition to be a purely physical disorder and disregarded the
demonic diagnosis of his fellow-countrymen?
The difficulty, however, is that apart from the highly in-
conclusive evidence of Matthew 4:24, one looks in vain for
any clear example of specifically *mental* illness which is *not*
ascribed to demons and which is cured by any means other
than exorcism. This observation has led some to speculate
that demonic activity was much more concentrated in
Christ's day than it is in ours, either because his unique
messianic presence provoked it, or because the power of the
kingdom of God had not yet been fully released into the
world to oppose it.

But were there really no examples of non-demonic psy-
chosis or epilepsy in first-century Palestine at all? If such
conditions existed, why do we not find Jesus healing them
by touch in the same way he heals other organic disorders?
A more plausible interpretation of the New Testament evidence must surely be that *all* illness in Jesus' day which was
accompanied by irrational or bizarre behaviour was regularly attributed to demonic involvement.

Extra-biblical sources provide little information about
medical practice and diagnosis in the Middle East in this period that might help to confirm this. However, if a non-
supernaturalist interpretation deriving from physicians in
the Greek Hippocratic tradition was available in first century Palestine, it does not seem to have percolated into
popular culture, and there is certainly no clear evidence of
it in the gospels. Where a secularised vocabulary of mental
illness is found, it is used in parallel with 'demonic' language in a way that suggests that the words do not represent
a rival anti-supernaturalist aetiology. A mentally-ill person

was simultaneously 'mad' and 'demon-possessed'. No evidence of the dualistic view that seeks to apply these terms to different phenomena can be found until many centuries later than Jesus.

Did Jesus in his healing ministry then simply accommodate himself to this cultural situation, in the same way that he sends a cleansed leper to the priest (Matthew 8:4) or uses saliva to anoint blind eyes (John 9:6)?

Liberal commentators often assume that the biblical vocabulary of possession is a dispensable facet of first century culture which needs to be demythologised for a modern western audience. Such a view is open to major objections. The objective reality of the demons Jesus expels seems to be confirmed both by their apparently supernatural recognition of his messianic identity and their bizarre transfer on one extraordinary occasion into a herd of pigs (see Matthew 8:28–34). There is also an enormous amount of anecdotal testimony from church and missionary experience over the centuries that is hard to explain without recourse to the demonic model. Whilst it is true that much recent material of this sort derives from rather sensationalist sources, there has also been some careful and objective research done. John Richards' book *But Deliver Us from Evil* (1974) remains a classic piece of work in this regard.

Those who wish to affirm that demon possession is a real possibility have usually resorted to the traditional dualistic view, in spite of its slender base in New Testament exegesis. They have accordingly sought to argue that it is possible to distinguish it from other forms of mental illness, perhaps by the application of some diagnostic test (e.g. holy water or the pronouncement of Jesus' name), or on the grounds of involvement with the occult. The suggestion that the gift of 'discerning spirits' (1 Corinthians 12:10) refers to a supernatural ability to identify demonic involvement in illness is also common. John Richards argues that the diagnosis of demon possession should be based on a number of such clues: the rational elimination of other causes, an informed analysis of symptoms and case history, and the employment of charismatic intuition. But he accepts that it may not always be possible to come to a firm conclusion even so, and suggests that maybe it is not always important to do so. If conventional therapy has failed and exorcism works, then the assumption must be that exorcism was needed.

An Alternative Holistic Model

Rather than treating demon-possession as one kind of mental illness to be clinically or charismatically distinguished from psychoses and personality disorders arising from organic or psychodynamic causes in this *dualistic* fashion, it may be more consonant with a biblical understanding of the human personality to look for a different model of mental illness. . . .

An alternative *holistic* model . . . permits this. Thus mental illness might be caused by faulty body chemistry (physical influence), dysfunctional family experience (social influence), demonic assault (spiritual influence) or unresolved guilt (personal sin).

Equally, healing can be sought via any of these channels. Drug treatment, psychotherapy and exorcism should not be regarded as mutually incompatible remedies but as complementary therapeutic interventions, each exploiting a different facet of human nature. This is not to suggest that the organic, psychodynamic and demonic interpretations of mental illness are just different metaphors describing the same phenomenon. These are all real and distinct potential factors. Sometimes it will be possible to diagnose a single one of them as the initiating agent. Thus, for instance, X-ray identification of a brain tumour and its subsequent removal by surgery or radiotherapy may be the whole story in some cases. Alzheimer's Disease can similarly be attributed to entirely physiological causes. But the essential unity of human nature makes it likely that in many other cases the precise origin of mental illness will be indeterminate, perhaps involving several of these facets of the human personality simultaneously. The possibility of demonic involvement therefore ought always to be considered as one potential strand of diagnosis and of the subsequent therapeutic regime.

Implications for Biblical Interpretation

If this holistic model is accepted we can do justice to both modern science and the Bible without resorting either to artificial harmonisation or demythologising the text.

The Bible would not ascribe mental illness to demonic activity in the way it does if this were a totally mistaken idea. But equally, it is a fundamental hermeneutic blunder to treat biblical authors as if they had access to modern medical and scientific knowledge. They write infallibly, but within the limitations of their own culture and language. When it came to describing mental illness, this meant that the New Testament writers had no alternative but to reflect the universal preoccupation with evil spirits which was characteristic of their day. Thus when Luke reports that a woman had been crippled 'by a spirit' (13:11) or Matthew identifies a blind mute as 'demon-possessed' (12:22), we do not have to interpret them in such a way as to exclude the validity of non-supernatural medical diagnoses, had such been available at that time. Would the epileptic boy of Matthew 17 have responded to modern anti-convulsive medication? According to the holistic model there is no reason why not.

Does the fact that Jesus always used exorcism in cases of mental illness mean that he never encountered cases of organic brain disorder? On the holistic model we are not bound to come to such a conclusion. It is perfectly possible that Jesus was merely accommodating himself to the expectations of healing methodology which were current in his day. To admit this is not to demythologise all references to the demonic, but it is to seek to do justice to their cultural context. While Jesus clearly endorsed demon-possession as a valid description of mental illness, he was not necessarily implying that it was an exhaustive explanation. Indeed we now know that it is not.

Implications for Pastoral Practice

Many people today are dissatisfied with the hubris of modern medical science and are sympathetic towards more holistic forms of therapy. Christians ought to sympathise with this, even if they are wary of some of its New Age associations. In practice, however, it is only in Catholic and Pentecostal traditions that 'spiritual' healing has retained any kind of major profile. The main body of the Protestant church in the last two centuries has tended to relegate the demonic to the area of personal temptation, and leave medical science to deal with illness. In part, this has no doubt been a reaction against the fanaticism and superstition that has often accompanied interest in demonology among other Christian groups. But perhaps Protestants have conceded too much ground to naturalistic science in this area. A responsible application of the holistic model may enable us to reclaim the church as a *therapeutic* community at a strategic moment in our cultural history.

In practical pastoral terms the holistic model argues for an approach to the treatment of mental illness which is eclectic and integrated.

Mental illness is far more complex than the medical, psychodynamic or demonic models allow. Each of these models in isolation is potentially reductionist. We need an approach that integrates the insights of all three of these perspectives. It is clear that the Bible sees no contradiction in the simultaneous application of both medical and spiritual remedies to a sick person. Hezekiah applies a poultice to his boil and also prays for healing (Isaiah 38). James recommends anointing with oil, the intercession of the church elders and the confession of sin (5:14–16). Where physical illness is concerned we have no difficulty taking the pills the doctor prescribes and at the same time asking the church to pray for healing. Why then, in cases of mental illness, should the healing resources of medicine, psychotherapy, exorcism and gospel proclamation not be used together in a collaborative regime that affirms the validity of each within its own frame of reference?

The pastoral counselling of the mentally ill requires a sensitive appreciation of the fact that some people need to take drugs, perhaps indefinitely; some people need a long period of skilled psychotherapeutic counselling; some people need to be supernaturally delivered from inner bondage to evil forces; some people need to repent and believe the gospel; and some people need a combination of several or even all of these remedies.

This is not to recommend the uncritical adoption of every technique on offer. As far as exorcism in particular is concerned, it is important to note that the 'try it and see if it works' pragmatism advocated by some enthusiasts for deliverance ministry does have considerable dangers. The medical literature is not short of reports about patients whose condition was worsened by exorcism rituals. Merely to suggest to a mentally disturbed person that there may be demonic involvement in their condition could quite easily exacerbate their anxiety in a most unhelpful fashion. What is more, the rabid ranting and hysteria characteristic of some so-called Christian exorcists bears little similarity to the calm authority with which Jesus and the apostles handled such cases. If exorcism is to be reclaimed by Christians in the mainstream Protestant tradition, it will undoubtedly require the development of an approach which is far more responsible than that which prevails in much of the deliverance ministry scene at the moment.

Psychotherapy also requires a good deal of critical examination if it is to be satisfactorily incorporated into Christian counselling. Like exorcism, it sometimes results in the patient becoming more distressed rather than less, and a cathartic resolution is not always achieved. This field is also rife with eccentric forms of practice, much of it reflecting a humanistic worldview which is quite incompatible with the Bible. Once again the development of a theologically informed methodology is indispensable.

Exorcism and Theology

There may be a strong case, in fact, for commencing intervention as a general rule in the 'organic' channel. Medication rarely causes an irreversible worsening of the patient's condition, and it may well achieve an amelioration of the symptoms of mental or emotional disturbance. If nothing else, this may be a useful preliminary to other forms of therapy where the person's cognitive engagement with the counsellor or exorcist is highly desirable.

But of course the control of symptoms by drugs is not necessarily the same thing as a cure. If Christian pastors need to be far less suspicious than some are of the healing methods of contemporary psychiatry, then psychiatrists need to be less dismissive also of the therapeutic resources of the Christian church. Modern medicine has been only partially successful in the organic treatment of mental illness. While no doubt many advances have yet to be made,

Christians have every right to insist that moral and spiritual factors play a significant role in this kind of disorder. As C.S. Lewis observed in *The Screwtape Letters*, the Devil disguises his activity well and is as happy with the scepticism of the secularist as with the fanaticism of the occultist. Undoubtedly mental illness is not the only, or even the major, sphere of his activity in our modern world. But the New Testament indicates that the demonic contribution in this area should not be neglected. It would be encouraging to think that the integrated model proposed above could result in teams of Christian psychiatrists, psychotherapists, counsellors and pastors working together on the same cases. Such teams could offer an integrated approach to the treatment of mental illness, taking the phenomenon of spiritual evil seriously, without engendering the unhealthily obsessional attitude towards the demonic which in the past has too often undermined the credibility of healing ministry in the church.

As New Age ideas permeate Western culture, the spirit-world is being accorded a far greater degree of plausibility. A window of opportunity is thus being provided for Christians to demonstrate a biblical balance and confidence in handling demonic aspects of human experience. It would be tragic if the non-Pentecostal Protestant wing of the Church proved so wedded to the rationalist presuppositions of its post-Enlightenment roots that it was unable to respond to this challenge.

Exorcism Can Heal People

M. Scott Peck

The past thirty years have brought a growing demand for exorcists and a growing number of people who claim that exorcism has had a positive impact on their lives. Many psychiatrists and clinical psychologists agree that exorcism may be beneficial for patients who believe it to be valid. For example, the British Health Education Authority has officially acknowledged that "some people have found exorcism and similar approaches helpful." However, most psychiatrists question exorcism's long-term value as a form of therapy.

Here, psychiatrist M. Scott Peck—author of the bestselling *The Road Less Traveled* (1978)—describes two cases of exorcism he regards as successful and discusses the role of the exorcist in curing demonic possession. Peck believes that exorcism—when performed in a loving and humane way, and with respect for the patient's autonomy—can improve the lives of people who believe that they are afflicted by a demonic presence.

M. Scott Peck, *People of the Lie: The Hope for Healing Human Evil*. New York: Simon & Schuster, Inc., 1983. Copyright © 1983 by M. Scott Peck, M.D. Reproduced by permission of the publisher.

[W]hen I began work on this book [*People of the Lie*] I could no longer avoid the issue of the demonic. . . . Writing directly on the subject of evil was another matter, however. Having come over the years to a belief in the reality of benign spirit, or God, and a belief in the reality of human evil, I was left facing an obvious intellectual question: Is there such a thing as evil spirit? Namely, the devil?

I thought not. In common with 99 percent of psychiatrists and the majority of clergy, I did not think the devil existed. Still, priding myself on being an open-minded scientist, I felt I had to examine the evidence that might challenge my inclination in the matter. It occurred to me that if I could see one good old-fashioned case of possession I might change my mind.

Of course I did not believe that possession existed. In fifteen years of busy psychiatric practice I had never seen anything faintly resembling a case. Admittedly, for the first ten of those years I might, with my prejudice, have walked right over one and not known it. . . .

But the fact that I had never seen a case did not mean such cases, past or present, were out of the question. I had discovered a large volume of literature on the subject— none of it "scientific." Much of it seemed naïve, simplistic, shoddy, or sensational. A few authors, however, seemed thoughtful and sophisticated, and they invariably stated that genuine possession was a very rare phenomenon. I therefore could not assume it to be unreal on the basis of limited experience.

So I decided to go out and look for a case. I wrote around and let it be known that I was interested in observing cases of purported possession for evaluation. Referrals trickled in.

The first two cases turned out to be suffering from standard psychiatric disorders, as I had suspected, and I began making marks on my scientific pistol. The third case turned out to be the real thing. Since then I have also been deeply involved with another case of genuine possession. In both cases I was privileged to be present at their successful exorcisms. The vast majority of cases described in the literature are those of possession by minor demons. These two were highly unusual in that both were cases of Satanic possession. I now know Satan is real. I have met it. . . .

Exorcism as Psychotherapy

One might think of exorcism and psychotherapy as utterly different, mutually exclusive approaches. The two exorcisms I witnessed, however, both seemed to me to be psychotherapeutic processes—in method as well as outcome. Indeed, a week after one exorcism, the patient, who had been seeing psychiatrists for many years, exclaimed, "All psychotherapy is a kind of exorcism!" And in my experience, all good psychotherapy does in fact combat lies.

The differences between psychoanalytic psychotherapy and exorcism fall into two categories: conceptual frames of reference and the use of power.

Almost innumerable volumes have been written about the conceptual frames of reference of Christianity and psychoanalysis, and it is not now appropriate to delve more deeply into the subject. What is appropriate is to point out that these frames of reference need not be mutually exclusive. I have been combining them in various mixtures in ordinary psychotherapy for some years with many patients and apparently with considerable success. Increasing numbers of other therapists have been doing likewise.

As to the use of power, psychoanalytic psychotherapy and

exorcism are *radically* different. Traditional psychotherapy—whether it be psychoanalytically oriented or not—deliberately makes little or no use whatsoever of power. It is conducted in an atmosphere of total freedom. The patient is free to quit therapy at any time. Indeed, he or she is free to leave even in the middle of a session. . . . Except for the threat of refusing to see the patient anymore (which is virtually never a constructive maneuver) the therapist has no weapons with which to push for change beyond the persuasive power of his or her own wits, understanding, and love.

Exorcism is another matter. Here the healer calls upon every power that is legitimately, lovingly available in the battle against the patient's sickness. First of all, exorcism, as far as I know, is always conducted by a team of at least three or more. In a sense the team "gangs up" on the patient. Unlike traditional therapy, in which it is one "against" one, in exorcism the patient is outnumbered.

The Means of Exorcism

The length of an exorcism session is not preset but is at the discretion of the team leader. In ordinary psychotherapy the session is no more than an hour, and the patient knows this. If they want to, patients can evade almost any issue for an hour. But exorcism sessions may last three, five, even ten or twelve hours—as long as the team feels is required to confront the issue. Also, the patient may be forcefully restrained during an exorcism session—and, indeed, frequently is—which is one of the reasons for the team approach. He or she cannot . . . walk out whenever things get unpleasant.

Finally—and most important—the exorcism team, through prayer and ritual, invokes the power of God in the healing process. For the nonbeliever this may seem like an ineffective measure, or else its effectiveness would be explained in terms of the mere power of suggestion. Speaking as a believer, I can only offer my personal experience of the presence of God in the room during the exorcisms I witnessed. Indeed, as far as the Christian exorcist is concerned, it is not he or she who successfully completes the process; it is God who does the healing. The whole purpose of the prayer and ritual is to bring the power of God into the fray. So it is that exorcism is seen by its practitioners in terms of spiritual warfare. The strategy is not, one hopes, that "all is fair in war." But the exorcist does believe it is legitimate to use any and every loving means—to ask for any loving help and use any loving resource—that can be summoned or otherwise made available in the battle.

The key word is "loving."

A Dangerous Procedure

Because it not only condones but insists on the use of power, I consider exorcism to be a dangerous procedure. Power is always subject to misuse. But the simple fact of its potential danger is hardly reason to outlaw it. The four-hour neurosurgical procedure that I underwent three years ago to relieve the pressure of disc and bone on the spinal cord in my neck was dangerous; it also made it possible for me to be writing these very words this very moment instead of being a bedridden quadriplegic or insane with chronic pain. From my vantage point, exorcism stands in relation to ordinary psychotherapy as radical surgery does to lancing a boil. Radical surgery can be not only healing but lifesaving, and, in fact, may be the only way to heal in certain cases unresponsive to more conservative therapy.

One issue to be considered in relation to the use of power in exorcism is that of brainwashing. I have struggled with this issue and have concluded that exorcism is indeed a form of brainwashing. One individual whose exorcism I witnessed was highly ambivalent after the procedure—simultaneously feeling relieved, profoundly grateful, and raped. In the years since then the feelings of gratitude and relief have, if anything, increased, and the sense of rape has faded—as does the trauma of surgery.

What prevents exorcism from being true rape is that, as with surgery, the individual consents to the procedure. One safeguard against the misuse of power in exorcism is to bear in mind the extreme importance of this issue of consent. I suspect some exorcists consider it too lightly. And perhaps one thing we practitioners of traditional medicine and surgery can contribute to exorcism is an insistence on "informed consent." So it is that before surgery we will formally and legally read patients their rights—or rather a list of rights they are consenting to forfeit. During the procedure of exorcism patients forfeit a great deal of their freedom. I firmly believe this forfeiture should be under legal conditions and conducted in a legal manner. Before the procedure patients should sign not simple but elaborate authorization forms. They should know exactly what they are letting themselves in for. And if a patient is clearly incapable of such awareness, a guardian should be legally appointed to make a reasoned decision for him or her.

Other safeguards should be employed as well. An objective record should be kept of the proceedings which can be made public if the patient or guardian desires. At the very least, this record should be an audiotape. Preferably it should be a videotape. A relative should be present if one suitably detached can be found.

"Very High Voltages"

But the greatest safeguard is love. Only with love can exorcists discern between interventions that are "fair" and necessary and those that are manipulative or truly violating. Only with love can practitioners be sure to keep the patients' best interests in mind at all times and be certain of resisting the omnipresent human tendency to become unscrupulous and enamored with power. Indeed, in all serious cases more is required than knowledge and skill; it is only love that can heal.

Exorcism is not a magical procedure—unless one considers love to be magical. As in psychotherapy, it makes use of analysis, of careful discernment, of interpretation, of encouragement, and of loving confrontation. It differs from traditional psychotherapy only as open-heart surgery differs from a tonsillectomy. Exorcism is psychotherapy by massive assault.

Like any massive assault, it is potentially quite dangerous and should be used only in cases so severe that lesser varieties of psychotherapy are doomed to failure. Moreover, it should be regarded as an experimental procedure until it has been scientifically investigated. In exorcism one is dealing with very high voltages.

The whole purpose of an exorcism is to uncover and isolate the demonic within the patient so that it can then be expelled. The demonic can have a tremendous energy of its own. Perhaps there are cases in which this energy is too powerful for either the patient or the team to cope with. Or the patient may not truly desire to be rid of it. Then the outcome of an exorcism would probably leave the patient worse off than before. The result could conceivably even be fatal. In such cases it would be better if the "high voltage" demonic energy had never been tapped into or uncovered in the first place. Before both exorcisms in which I participated, the patients signed consent forms acknowledging their awareness that the exorcism might fail and that they might even die as a result of the procedure. (This should give the reader some notion of their courage and desperation.)

Risks to the Exorcists

Then there is the danger to the exorcist and the other team members. . . . But the psychological dangers are real and enormous. Both the exorcisms I witnessed were successful. I shudder to think what the effect would have been on the exorcist or other team members—on me—if they had failed. Even though all team members had been carefully chosen for their psychological strength as well as their love, the procedures were stressful for everyone. And even though the outcome was successful, most had emotional reactions to contend with in the weeks afterward.

I might add that exorcism is not what one would ordinarily think of as a "cost effective" procedure. The first (and easier) required a team of seven highly trained professionals to work (without payment) four days, twelve to sixteen hours a day. The second involved a similar team, of nine men and women, who worked twelve to twenty hours a day for three days. Not that it is necessarily always such a massive undertaking. I remind the reader that both cases were apparently unusual in being Satanic possession.

Difficult and dangerous though they were, the exorcisms I witnessed were successful. I cannot imagine how otherwise the two patients could have been healed. They are both alive and very well today. I have every reason to believe that had they not had their exorcisms they would each be dead by now.

Exorcism Saves People from Evil Forces

Francis MacNutt

Within the evangelical Protestant Christian tradition, the concept of exorcism as a formal ritual has given way to *deliverance*—the casting out of demons as a form of ministry. Depending on the severity of the demonic threat, deliverance ministry can be as physical as traditional exorcism or as noninvasive as prayer.

In this excerpt from his book *Deliverance from Evil Spirits: A Practical Manual*, Francis MacNutt—a former Roman Catholic priest who serves as director of Christian Healing Ministries—describes the role of a deliverance minister. MacNutt argues that the ministry of deliverance, which is difficult and must be undertaken with great caution, serves a vital and necessary role in protecting human beings from evil forces.

The first and most common way we find out that a person needs deliverance is that he tells us. Affected people usually know not only that something is wrong, but that their problem might be caused by evil spirits.

We do not necessarily believe what people tell us, of course. I remember a high school student brought to me by a group of priests who said he exhibited all the signs of demonic infestation when they prayed for him. Fortunately Dr. Conrad Baars, the Christian psychiatrist, was visiting me at the time and sat in on the interview. In a skilled way Dr. Baars asked the boy a number of questions. Finally, after an hour, the boy admitted he had faked all this behavior because he was lonely and wanted to attract attention.

People genuinely afflicted by evil spirits are usually loath to talk about their problem and are often afraid even to tell their friends or counselor, much less their minister or priest, because they fear they will be written off as unbalanced or, worse yet, psychotic.

I have found, though, that many people really seem to experience evil, either from within themselves (demonization) or from without (oppression), and they do need help in being freed.

Experiencing Demonic Infestation

They experience evil in all sorts of ways. Some hear voices, which typically impel them toward suicide or hate (especially hatred of themselves): "Drive your car off the road into that tree! Now!" "You're no damn good. You are condemned to hell forever." "You belong to me and you will never escape." These are common messages I hear from the afflicted again and again.

Others see visions or have nightmares that seem more real and convey more terror than ordinary nightmares. Still others feel impelled to do things they would never ordinarily think of doing.

No matter how this demonic control manifests itself, a significant number of people will tell you—if they feel you will listen and can help—that something is radically wrong and that they believe evil spirits are involved.

We realize, of course, that they may be wrong; they may simply be deluded or they may be hallucinating and suffering psychotic episodes. They may be more in need of a psychiatrist or counselor than of someone who can pray for their deliverance.* It goes without saying that we need to understand this and not take everything people say at face value. But we need to be open to the person who asks for help, believing he is under demonic attack.

It usually takes courage for people to tell us they think they may be under demonic influence. Do not subject them, first of all, to skepticism or, worse yet, scoffing. You will need to sort out whether their conviction is true. But take it seriously. If you begin by reacting skeptically, they will probably clam up.

Many of the deliverances we perform start out with a conversation in which the victimized person gives us the right discernment about where the problem lies.

For me this has been the most common way I have discovered the need to pray for deliverance: The person I am praying with starts to act in a strange way that indicates an evil spirit is present. . . .

The strongest signs are bodily contortions, changes in the voice and changes in facial expression.

Bodily Contortions

We read in the New Testament about such phenomena: "The evil spirit shook the man violently" (Mark 1:26) and

---

*The psychiatrists and counselors I work with also believe in prayer for inner healing and deliverance and include prayer as part of their practice.

"He would cry out and cut himself with stones" (Mark 5:5). At times—for instance, when the spirit of death is present—the person grows rigid, especially around the fingers. Other people may arch their spines backward, while still others roll on the ground. One man started leaping around like a tiger and jumped up on the back of the couch as if to pounce on me. (I commanded him in the name of Jesus not to jump and he was immobilized.) Another man got down on all fours and started roaring like a lion, while at the same meeting a woman dropped off her chair and started slithering on the floor like a snake.

These examples may sound bizarre to someone who has never seen someone being freed from the effects of witchcraft, but they happen frequently in our ministry. Fortunately, most of the bodily contortions we see are not so violent.

The Voice

Sometimes the *tone* of the person's voice changes. A woman may start speaking in a husky voice like a man, or a mild-mannered person may begin speaking in a snide, insulting tone of voice.

Sometimes the *content* of what the person says changes and indicates the influence of a spirit. I have already mentioned that the person may start speaking in the plural *we* instead of *I*: "We are not going to leave."

When the voice changes, the content usually changes, too. In Japan a woman who did not speak English said, in English, to a priest on our team who was praying with her, "I'd like to sleep with you."

Other Effects

The Face

Perhaps the most common external indication of demonization comes when the person's facial expression changes. It is as if you are no longer looking at the same person you started talking to. The old saying "The eyes are the windows of the soul" becomes especially meaningful. It is as if the evil spirit is peering out at you. The eyes become filled with hate, mockery, pride or whatever the nature of that particular spirit is. Now that the evil spirit has surfaced, you are no longer directly in touch with the person you have been praying for.

Sometimes the eyes roll upwards, so that all you can see are the whites of the eyes—a weird effect. (This seems to be the spirit's way of avoiding looking at you, in an effort to keep the victim from making contact with you and getting help.)

Other Clues

Some of these dramatic examples are evident only in a person who suffers from severe demonization. Again, notice that all these signs are ambiguous; psychological problems can account for many similar extraordinary gestures. Yet when you see these signs, be aware that you may be watching the effects of demonic activity and may need eventually to pray for the person's liberation, or refer the person to someone with more experience.

A significant aspect of these strange activities is that they occur consistently. Facial expressions, bodily contortions and vocal statements caused by evil spirits are remarkably similar, even though most of the people we work with have never read in detail about such activity or seen it in anyone else. (In the United States we see the same symptoms as in Africa or Japan.) It is one more indication that we are truly dealing with demonic forces.

When Judith [MacNutt's wife] worked in Jerusalem she became convinced of the reality of the demonic world when she saw contortions, together with vocal and facial changes, in many of the people she prayed with, regardless of whether they came from Christian, Jewish or Muslim backgrounds. (Later, in fact, a spirit speaking through a woman we were praying for in Florida said to Judith, "I met you before in Jerusalem!")

Some other signs of demonic presence include unpleasant smells and, above all, cold. When the Holy Spirit is present we often experience heat. (I usually need to take off my sweater when we pray.) But when an evil spirit is present the room grows cold.

After you have had a certain amount of experience in the deliverance ministry, you will learn to recognize many of these familiar signs of demonic presence. They enable you to say to yourself, *I think we're faced with an evil spirit here.*

Possession or MPD?

A special area of concern is Multiple Personality Disorder (MPD, also known as DID, Dissociative Identity Disorder). Since the external symptoms of the need for deliverance are ambiguous, we must ask what is causing the symptoms, a psychiatric disorder or a demon. If we are not sure, we need to proceed gently and with caution.

> Rolling eyes, voice changes, twitches, or marked shifts in facial expression could indicate either. . . . Exorcists likely have not known enough about MPD to tell the difference. . . . Christians who have had years of experience in deliverance work say they knew all along that certain entities seemed like demons initially but didn't respond to exorcism like demons do.[1]

The worst thing you can do, if the person does have various personalities (needed in order to survive), is try to cast them out. Just this week an MPD client visited here devastated and confused because a female minister had sat on her physically and tried to perform an exorcism. This kind of well-meaning but ignorant ministry further fragments the person and gives exorcism a bad name in the psychiatric and counseling professions.

If anger emerges unexpectedly and the person you are

working with suddenly acts like an entirely different personality, how can you be sure what you are working with?
The most accurate way of diagnosing the presence of an
evil spirit is through the gift of discerning spirits (which we
will discuss next). Apart from that, I encourage you to read
a reputable book about MPD that takes into account the reality of the need for deliverance. One such book is *Uncovering the Mystery of MPD*, in which Dr. James Friesen writes:

> It can be easy to misdiagnose dissociations. When a differ-
> ent alter takes executive control of the body, the process is
> often accompanied by a change in posture—a twitch, a
> blink, or a blackout, for example. It is understandable that
> some people could misinterpret the postural change as an
> evil spirit taking control. Whenever such a dissociation is
> treated as possession, I would call that religious abuse. . . .
> Alters cannot be erased, and they cannot be cast out. Life
> takes a plunge if that is attempted. Religious abuse can cause
> even more hurt than therapeutic abuse.[2]

Clearly, whenever possible you should get to know the
person you are going to pray with and really listen to what
he says. Do not force him to interpret his experience according to your understanding. MPD clients have been victims of severe trauma (usually in childhood) and can be set
free from demons of trauma if you pray for Jesus to heal
them of these traumas. This gentle approach, if you are not
sure what you are dealing with, bypasses the problem of
getting involved too quickly in a direct confrontation.

The Gift of Discerning Spirits

One of the gifts the Holy Spirit gives us to build up the Christian community is the ability to discern spirits. This gift of
recognizing spirits is the seventh of the nine spiritual manifestations listed by Paul in 1 Corinthians 12:8–10. Discernment is the God-given ability to know, on occasion, whether
an evil spirit is present. This gift enables us to distinguish

whether a person (or his actions) is influenced primarily by
1. the *Holy* Spirit;
2. *natural,* human, psychological or created causes;
3. an *evil* spirit.

Without discernment, when we are faced with the signs we have been talking about (signs like changes in the voice), we must try to deduce the presence of a spirit from what people say or how they act. We are merely using our minds to argue from an effect (for example, a man convulsing on the ground) to the possible cause. We can make a good guess about the diagnosis, but unless God helps us in some way, we can never be certain what we are dealing with.

When a person has the gift of discernment, on the other hand, he is able to come closer to certainty. The only difficulty is that this wonderful gift of discernment does not seem to be fully developed in many people.

In general, we need not accept the discernment of a person unless we know him well—one of the reasons we need an established Christian community and colleagues we know and trust.

In talking to friends whom I believe have this ability to discern spirits, I find that discernment operates on two levels:
1. the ability to recognize the *presence* of an evil spirit;
2. the additional ability (at a higher level) to know the *identity* or name of the evil spirit.

Recognizing the Presence of a Spirit

Simply being able to recognize that a spirit is present is a considerable spiritual gifting. This ability comes to people in all sorts of ways. Just as a fairly large number of people "see" angels, a number can also see evil spirits (fallen angels). Some of my friends see the spirits with a kind of spiritual vision in ministry situations when they start praying for guidance or healing.

Different people sense the presence of evil spirits in different ways. One evangelist has learned that when he feels the hair on the back of his neck stand up, a demon is present. Another friend, Dr. Robert Lindsey, long-time pastor of the Narkiss Street Baptist Church in Jerusalem, has come to recognize that when his right earlobe tingles in a certain way, an evil spirit is present. Still another friend smells an unusual, unpleasant odor when evil spirits are around. When St. Catherine of Siena visited the papal court in Avignon, France, she was overwhelmed by the stench she found there, and attributed the odor to sin and demons rather than to natural causes. Other people simply sense in some inexplicable way that an evil spirit is near.

Some of these ways of discerning, as you can see, are highly singular and require some experience to interpret rightly. But those who detect evil (like a smoke detector warning us of fire) say there is something unusual in the way they sense evil that alerts them to the fact that it is not a purely natural phenomenon. If you *smell* the presence of evil, for example, it is like nothing you have ever smelled before; it is as distinctive as the smell of Limburger cheese.

Regardless of the form that discernment takes, it certainly helps to be able to walk into a situation (sometimes one that appears innocent) and know immediately that something evil lies beneath the surface. At the very least, you are being warned to watch out, to be wary about what this person says or does. At most, God may be calling you to pray for a deliverance that will free the sufferer.

Discerning the Identity of the Spirit

If it is a great help to know when an evil spirit is present, it is even more useful to know the spirit's nature and identity. The clearest discernment seems to come, again, through spiritual sight, "seeing" what the spirit looks like, combined with a direct spiritual insight into its name or nature. Knowing the spirit's name (for example, the spirit of lust) seems to give us a power over the spirit that helps us cast it out.

When I am praying for a person for healing, it helps to have someone by my side who has the ability to discern spirits. If the person I am praying for starts to exhibit behavior indicating that a spirit is present, I will ask my colleague to tell me what we are dealing with.

Like all gifts of the Spirit, this one needs to be tested. I do not have to believe every person who tells me he discerns that a particular evil spirit is present. Again, this is one of the reasons we need a community in which we have time to recognize and test the gifts that the Holy Spirit gives to different people to benefit the Church.

Some may have a strong gift of prophecy, healing or discerning of spirits but contaminate it, if they are immature in its use, with elements of their own prejudice, self-interest or religious background. A prophetic message may, at least in part, be from God but mixed with personal opinion, because the person has listened to his own heart and desires and has mistaken that for the Lord.

The Team

Thus, unless we ourselves have the gift of discernment, it is important to know the people we work with. I know several people whom I trust because of our past common experience; they always seem to be right on.

The people I know who not only recognize when an evil spirit is present, but can identify the spirit's identity or nature (e.g., "A spirit of death is in this room"), receive this information in a variety of ways. Some "see" the spirits and recognize them from having seen and identified them on previous occasions. Others pick up a kind of spiritual or mental apprehension of the spirit's identity, perhaps through a thought or word that comes to them, like *hatred*. Learning the identity of the spirit we are facing is helpful because it gives us a clue as to how the spirit entered the afflicted person. This avenue needs to be closed through either repentance or inner healing. If you find you are dealing with lust, for example, the person probably needs to repent of past behavior. If you discover that rejection or grief is the spirit coming to the fore, it is likely that inner healing is needed to heal the traumas of rejection and grief that have left a spiritual wound. A tormenting spirit has moved into that wound and continues to inflame it.

An authentic ability to discern spirits given by the Holy Spirit is the quickest, most accurate way of getting the diagnosis we need to decide how best to proceed. The key word here is *authentic* because, at least according to my experience, a finely tuned, mature gift of discernment is relatively rare. The reason for this, I believe, is that churches have neglected the deliverance ministry, and those people God might have called into a deliverance ministry have not had a chance to exercise or grow into their spiritual gifts.

Zealous Christians who *have* gotten into deliverance, on the other hand, have usually received insufficient instruction or oversight to direct a balanced ministry. The most common problem we find is that some ministers of deliverance know little about psychology and are unable to tell whether a person needs inner healing or deliverance or both. Right now, for example, a psychiatrist friend is treating a client who went to a ministry that tried to cast demons out of her. When she got no better, they thrust her further into the pit of self-hatred by blaming her for not getting well. Such unbalanced ministry has given exorcism a bad name in the medical and counseling professions, as well as in the mainline churches.

A Necessary Ministry

But the answer to abuse is not to shut down the deliverance ministry. The answer is not *no* use but *right* use.

The problems that turn up (and everyone has heard about them) simply serve as an excuse for denial by many Christian ministers unwilling to recognize a more important problem: that many people suffer from demonic infestation and that there is an enormous vacuum in pastoral practice because most churches are not dealing with demonic infestation.

Yet even without a clear gift of discernment, the ordinary signs indicating that an evil spirit is present are often sufficient to allow us to minister with practical certitude.

Notes

1. James Friesen, Ph.D., *Uncovering the Mystery of MPD* (San Bernardino: Here's Life Publishers, 1991), p. 246.

2. Ibid., p. 107.

Chapter 2

Fact or Fiction?

Evidence Against
Possessions and
Exorcisms

Demonic Possession Cases Can Be Explained by Cultural Factors

Michael W. Cuneo

Most agree that a new surge of interest in possession and exorcism came about shortly after the success of the film *The Exorcist* (1973), but there is a great deal of disagreement about why this happened. Did *The Exorcist* actually bring about new cases of "demonic possession," or simply call more attention to a supernatural problem that has always existed?

In this article, Michael W. Cuneo—professor of sociology at Fordham University (a Jesuit institution) and author of *American Exorcism* (2001)—argues that the increase in exorcisms can be attributed to their well-marketed cultural appeal. Demonic possession is a fast and inexpensive diagnosis that allows its purported victims to blame their maladies

Michael W. Cuneo, "Exorcism: What the Devil Is Going On?" *U.S. Catholic*, vol. 67, October 2002, p. 35. Copyright © 2002 by *U.S. Catholic*. Reproduced by permission.

on demons (which can be exorcised) rather than on other factors (which can't). In the view of its proponents, exorcism is a treatment based on faith and love for those suffering from psychological or emotional problems.

Over the past several years I have discovered a side of America I never knew existed. In the course of intensive and far-flung research, I have sat in on dozens of exorcisms—not just Roman Catholic exorcisms but a wide variety of Protestant ones also. I have met with hundreds of people from various walks of life who are convinced not only that demons exist but also that they routinely cause trouble in the lives of ordinary women and men.

Standing at the back of an auditorium in suburban Chicago, I have seen several hundred impeccably groomed, middle-class Americans writhing and shrieking and groaning (some simulating masturbation) while attempting to free themselves from demons of sexual perversity. At a drab medical complex on the outskirts of Boston, I have watched an avuncular physician exorcising spirits of guilt and self-hatred from one of his patients. At several conservative Protestant churches in the Midwest, I have observed people retching and cursing and flinging themselves violently to the floor while being delivered of entire squadrons of demons.

I have received numerous invitations to undergo exorcism myself, once from two Episcopalians who wanted to shackle me to the support beams of a rural shed so my demons would depart peaceably. I have observed people at high-toned suburban churches vomiting profusely into trash containers while being purged of their evil spirits. I have heard fabulous accounts (from apparently sincere and lucid people) of gyrating heads, levitating bodies, and navel-licking tongues.

I have interviewed psychiatrists charged with the responsibility of evaluating suspected cases of demonic possession for the Catholic Church in the United States. And, not least of all, I have personally encountered more varieties of Catholic exorcism—official Catholic exorcism, bootleg Catholic exorcism, you-name-it Catholic exorcism—than I ever imagined existed.

The Rise of Exorcism in America

As unlikely as it may sound, exorcism is alive and well in contemporary America. It's a booming business—operating below the radar perhaps, invisible to anyone not specifically on the lookout for it, but booming nevertheless. Untold numbers of Americans, many of them staunchly middle-class—people you might chat with at the supermarket checkout counter—have undergone exorcisms of one kind or another, and many claim to have come out much the better for it.

It wasn't long ago, however, that almost nothing of this sort was going on in the United States. As recently as the late 1960s, exorcism was all but dead and forgotten—a fading ghost long past its prime. By the mid-'70s, however, the ghost had sprung miraculously back to life. Suddenly, countless people were convinced that they themselves, or perhaps a loved one, were suffering from demonic affliction, and exorcism was in hot demand.

What brought this about? A number of factors, but none more important, especially where Catholic exorcism is concerned, than the release of William Peter Blatty's *The Exorcist*—the book in 1971 and the movie two years later—and the publication in 1976 of Malachi Martin's demon-busting pulp classic *Hostage to the Devil*.

As if by alchemy, the dramatic (and seductively grotesque) arrival of demons on the screen and the bestselling page resulted in demons rampaging through the bedrooms and workplaces of Middle America. The pop culture industry cast its spell, so to speak, and an obliging nation fell into line. New exorcism ministries were brought into being to deal with the sudden onslaught of demonism, and older ministries were rejuvenated and found themselves with more business than they could possibly handle.

"A Thoroughly American Arrangement"

In a sense, the real curiosity isn't that exorcism is still practiced in contemporary America, but that it isn't practiced more widely. It would be difficult, after all, to imagine a better deal. Whatever one's personal problem—depression, anxiety, substance addiction, or even a runaway sexual appetite—there are exorcism ministries available today that will happily claim expertise for dealing with it, with the significant bonus that one is not, for the most part, held personally responsible for the problem. Indwelling demons are mainly to blame, and getting rid of them is the key to moral and psychological redemption. Personal engineering through demon-expulsion: a bit messy perhaps, but relatively fast and cheap, and morally exculpatory. A thoroughly American arrangement.

And this is precisely the point. In addition to being influenced by the popular entertainment industry, the practice of exorcism in contemporary America is remarkably well-suited to the therapeutic ethos of the prevailing culture. Exorcism ministries offer their clients endless possibilities for personal transformation. With its promises of therapeutic well-being and rapid-fire emotional gratification, exorcism is oddly at home in the purchase-of-happiness culture of turn-of-the-century America.

While fascinating in its own right, evangelical and charismatic "deliverance ministry" never really succeeded during the 1980s in capturing the imagination of the broader American public. For big-league wallop there was still no substitute, apparently, for exorcisms officially sanctioned by the Catholic Church and performed by bona fide hero-priests under the direction of their bishops. Although few and far between, these were the exorcisms the popular media feasted on, the inescapable standard by which all other forms of exorcism were measured. By almost universal consensus this was the genuine article, the truly epic struggle between supernatural good and evil. Everything else was pale imitation. . . .

But Does It Work?

Does exorcism, when all is said and done, actually deliver on its promises? Does it bring relief or freedom or wholeness? And—the million-dollar question—does it really deliver people from demons?

It's the demons I'm most often asked about. A wide variety of people—some deeply religious, some not religious in the least—want to know about the demons. Some of them take up a tone of self-protective irony, but they still want to know. They're genuinely curious—and they're half hoping I'll confirm what they've heard only from Hollywood. They're half hoping I'll tell them something juicy, something outrageous—something they'd never admit to believing. Most of all, they want to know this: Does exorcism really work as it's advertised? Does it really succeed in driving out . . . demons?

The truth is, I don't know about the demons. I've personally witnessed more than 50 exorcisms, and I still don't know.

At the exorcisms I attended, there were no spinning

heads, no levitating bodies, no voices from beyond the grave. There was plenty of vomiting, no question about it, but nothing more impressive than what you'd probably catch most Saturday nights out behind your local bar. I wasn't counting on demonic fireworks, but neither was I counting them out. After all was said and done, more than 50 exorcisms—no fireworks, none at all.

Occasionally I found myself in a situation where I was the odd man out, the party pooper of all party poopers. Just about everyone else on hand would claim to see something extraordinary, and they'd be disappointed that I hadn't seen it also. "You must have seen the body rising. The rest of us saw it. It clearly rose two, maybe three feet off the chair. How could you not have seen it?"

"I'm sorry, but I didn't see it. I was looking as hard as I could, and I didn't see it."

No, I didn't see it, and the reason I didn't? There was nothing to be seen. People tend to be so keyed up during an exorcism, so eager to sink their fingers into something preternatural, that they easily persuade themselves they're seeing, hearing, or feeling things that simply aren't really there to be seen, heard, or felt.

As for myself—open-mindedly skeptical, skeptically open-minded—I was ready for any kind of action, but I was determined not to fall into the trap of conjuring things up just to suit the mood of the occasion. What I saw (I'm quite sure) was actually there to be seen; what I didn't see . . . well, I'm afraid not.

The Placebo Effect

So what did I see? Some of the people who showed up for exorcisms seemed deeply troubled, some mildly troubled, and some hardly troubled at all. The symptoms they complained of—addictions and compulsions, violent mood swings, blurred self-identities, disturbing visions and somatic sensations—all of this seemed to me fully explainable in social, cultural, medical, and psychological terms. There seemed no compelling need whatsoever to bring demons into the equation.

The same with the antics I sometimes witnessed while the exorcisms were actually taking place, the flailing and slithering, the shrieking and moaning, the grimacing and growling—none of this, insofar as I could tell, suggested the presence of demons. It was sometimes an attempt to satisfy the dramatic needs of the moment, sometimes an exercise in sheer self-indulgence, and sometimes an indication of profound personal distress. But demons? Here again, I saw no evidence, nothing that had me itching to make a break for the door.

Some of the people I met during my research claimed to have experienced significant improvement in their personal lives as a result of undergoing exorcism. I have no way of knowing how extensive this improvement was, or how long-lived, or whether the people who told me about it were always telling the truth. But let's say, for the sake of argument, that they were telling the truth, and that their exorcisms really did have positive therapeutic impact. How can we account for this? Well, it's quite possible that exorcism sometimes works, but this need not have anything to do with the driving out of demons. What it has to do with, in all likelihood, is the placebo effect.

In psychotherapy—indeed, in virtually any medical procedure—the expectation of getting better may contribute a great deal to one's actually getting better. Simply receiving treatment—any kind, but especially treatment in a supportive healing environment—is the ticket at least partway home. The medical sciences have always strongly suspected that suggestion and expectancy are powerful inducements to healing, and today only the most hardened scissors-and-scalpel skeptic would argue otherwise.

Now, if placebos can be effective when administered in the relatively antiseptic confines of a doctor's office or a consultation room, imagine the possibilities in the emotional swelter-box of an exorcism.

"They Pray for It to Work"

Most people who seek out an exorcism are suffering from some psychological or emotional problem that they're convinced has been caused by demons. They believe that only through an exorcism will their problem be eliminated and their circumstances improved.

The person charged with performing the exorcism and the supporting cast of friends, family members, and assistants anticipate the same thing. All parties to the exorcism have an enormous investment in the affair: They want it to work, they expect it to work, they pray for it to work. And the symbolic universe they inhabit, with its shared religious meanings and discourse, demands that it work.

It doesn't always work, of course, but often enough (if only temporarily) it seems to. And little wonder—exorcism is a ritualized placebo, a placebo writ large, one that engages its participants on levels to which more conventional therapeutic procedures could scarcely aspire.

The Original Alternative Therapy

Here again, exorcism is more in tune with the times than one might imagine. In recent years increasing numbers of Americans have started experimenting with alternative medical therapies. Unhappy with the current state of the medical establishment—its impersonality, its technology, its bureaucratic chilliness—they've sought healing through the soothing remedies of herbalists, homeopaths, acupuncturists, diet gurus—you name it.

Though I wouldn't want to stretch the point too far, exorcism may be regarded as part of this scene, on its fringes perhaps, but part of it nonetheless. It, too, advertises a drug-free, X-ray-free, incision-free approach to restored health. It promises to mend not just the body and the mind but the soul as well. It's an alternative medical therapy for those who see demons, not cholesterol, not toxic particles, not environmental stress or genetic predisposition but rather real glowering, hell-bent-on-evil demons as the major scourge of our time.

In September 2000 a newly restored director's cut of *The Exorcist* was released to movie houses around the country. It was the cinematic event of the season, inciting yet another jag of media-obsessed demon-and-exorcism blather. For a solid month, or so it seemed, you couldn't pick up a newspaper, flip through a magazine, or turn on the television without coming up against it. More than a quarter century after Father Damien Karras first smoldered across the screen, exorcism was still sexy, still very much in demand, still panted after. It hadn't lost a thing.

Social Pressure Can Inspire Belief in Demonic Possession

Giuliana A.L. Mazzoni, Elizabeth F. Loftus, and Irving Kirsch

Both skeptics and believers generally agree that the number of exorcism cases seems to skyrocket whenever possession and exorcism are prominent in popular culture. While some believers argue that pop culture acceptance makes it easier for victims to find help, most skeptics claim that pop culture can be credited with creating the demonic possession phenomenon itself.

Experimental psychologists Giuliana A.L. Mazzoni, Elizabeth F. Loftus, and Irving Kirsch surveyed twenty-two Italian college students about the existence of demonic possession. They then subjected these students to materials and behav-

Giuliana A.L. Mazzoni, Elizabeth F. Loftus, and Irving Kirsch, "Changing Beliefs About Implausible Autobiographical Events: A Little Plausibility Goes a Long Way," *Journal of Experimental Psychology: Applied*, vol. 7, March 2001. Copyright © 2001 by the American Psychological Association. Reproduced by permission.

ior that would reinforce belief in demonic possession and, more specifically, belief that they had personally witnessed demonic possession as children. When the students were tested again, most were more open to the idea that possessions are real. By the end of the experiment, four students who had originally expressed skepticism came to believe that they had witnessed possession firsthand. From these results, the authors conclude that some people who believe they have witnessed demonic possession have in fact developed a false belief.

Many studies have shown that people can be led to believe that they experienced events, when in fact, they did not. People have been led to believe that they were born left-handed (*Kelley, Amodio, & Lindsay, 1996*), that they spilled punch at a wedding, (*Hyman, Husband, & Billings, 1995*), that they broke a window with their hand (*Garry, Manning, Loftus, & Sherman, 1996; Heaps & Nash, 1999*), or that they got lost before age 3 (*Mazzoni, Loftus, Seitz & Lynn, 1999*). These and other examples indicate how powerful suggestions can be in terms of making people believe that they had childhood experiences that they probably did not have.

It has been argued that there are limits to the types of events or beliefs that can be suggestively implanted, and that only events that are plausible can be implanted in memory. (*Hyman, Gilstrap, Decker, & Wilkinson, 1998; Hyman & Kleinknecht, 1999; Lindsay & Read, 1994; Pezdek, Finger, & Hodge, 1997*). In support of this hypothesis, *Pezdek et al. (1997)* reported successfully implanting a memory of being lost in 15% of participants, but being unable to implant a memory for a less plausible event (receiving a rectal enema). In a separate experiment (*Pezdek et al.*, *1997*), Jewish and Catholic participants received suggestions that as children, they had participated in Jewish Sabbath and a Catholic Communion. Participants were less susceptible to the suggestion that they had experienced a ritual foreign to their religion, rather than a ritual common to their religion. Only 3 of 29 Catholics (10%), and none of the Jewish participants, fell sway to the suggestion that they had participated in a foreign ritual, whereas larger percentages accepted the false suggestion that they had participated in a religion consistent ritual. Thus, the study showed that most participants resisted implausible suggestions.

Studies demonstrating the acceptance of false memory suggestions have been cited as indicative of the process by which false memories may be created in therapeutic and forensic settings (*Loftus, 1997; Mazzoni, in press*). However, some of the apparent memories created in these settings are for implausible events. People have not only developed memories for such implausible events as satanic ritual participation and alien abduction (*Mack, 1994*), but also for events that could not possibly be remembered, such as concrete narratives about the day after birth (*Spanos, Burgess, Burgess, Samuels, & Blois, 1999*). Given the data reported by *Pezdek et al. (1997)*, how is it that false memories for implausible events can be created? The solution to this dilemma resides in the recognition that the perceived plausibility of an event may not be fixed. We hypothesized that memories of implausible events were implanted in these cases because the specific individuals either (a) already believed that the events were plausible, or (b) were led to believe that those events were plausible. Thus, if an event is seen as more plausible, then this should pave the way for allowing its acceptance as having occurred.

We propose a three-step model for the development of

false memories. First, the event must be perceived as plausible. Second, individuals must acquire the autobiographical belief that it is likely to have happened to them. Third, individuals must interpret their thoughts and fantasies about the event as memories. This study is concerned with the first two of these three factors: perceived plausibility and the likelihood of the event having occurred to the person, as well as the relation between these two factors.

The purpose of this study was to test the hypotheses that (a) the perceived plausibility of an event can be changed by suggestive influence and (b) when plausibility is increased, further suggestive influence can increase ratings of the likelihood that an initially implausible event has occurred. Confirmation of these hypotheses would be consistent with the results of *Pezdek et al.* (1997), and would reconcile those data with data indicating the implantation of false memories for events generally seen as implausible. Thus, if we could make an event appear to be more plausible, then we would enhance the likelihood that a person might come to believe it was true for them personally.

The Experiment

In the first of three studies, people were recruited who (a) had not experienced the implausible event of witnessing another individual being "possessed" and (b) believed that such an experience was highly implausible. Much later during the second session of the study, some of these individuals were subjected to "plausibility" and "personalized suggestion" manipulations. For the plausibility manipulation, participants were provided with three mini-articles about possession, designed to enhance the subjective plausibility of possession and to increase the plausibility of the experience for each specific participants. The mini-articles gave information about the frequency of possession, suggesting it was more common than previously believed. The articles stressed the relative frequency of this phenomenon in the socioeconomic and cultural populations to which the participants belonged. Additionally, the articles provided stories, ostensibly experienced by other individuals, who had witnessed possession. After this plausibility manipulation (i.e., reading the articles), these participants went through a personalized suggestion procedure in which they took a test to measure their personal fears, and their "fear" data were interpreted as indicating that they may well have had the experience of witnessing possession. Finally, during the fourth and final session, participants rated the plausibility of witnessing possession, and indicated whether this had happened to them. To anticipate our results, we found that relative to controls, participants who received the intervening information came to believe that possession was more plausible and also increased their confidence that they had witnessed possession. . . .

There were several reasons for selecting the specific critical event (witnessing possession) for use in this research. First, belief in possession has emerged in the treatment of a number of therapy patients (*Loftus, 1997; Modi v. West Virginia Board of Medicine, 1995; Olson v. Morris, 1999*). Second, the participants in this research were young Italian adults. In Italian culture, the notion of possession is not so impossible as to be laughable, as would be, for example, the idea that your body turned forest green during your early childhood. However, possession is sufficiently implausible to be rated low in plausibility by most individuals. . . .

We examined the effects of a plausibility manipulation and a personalized suggestion on the perceived plausibility of an event and on ratings of the likelihood that it has occurred to the individual. Participants were divided into three groups. In one group, the manipulations were aimed at an initially implausible event (Witnessed Possession). In the second group the manipulations were aimed at an initially plausible event (Almost Choked). This allowed us to compare the effects of the suggestion on a naturally plausible event with the effects on an event whose plausibility had been experimentally enhanced. The third group received no experimental manipulation and provided a control for spontaneous changes in plausibility and likelihood ratings. We hypothesized that the manipulations would enhance the plausibility of the initially implausible event and would increase likelihood ratings for targeted events, regardless of whether they were initially plausible.

Method Participants.

Participants were 65 undergraduate students from the University of Florence, drawn from a larger pool of 430 students who had completed rating scales in a mass-testing session, and they were invited for further participation on the basis of their responses on the scales. Random assignment resulted in 12 women and 10 men in the Possession group, 13 women and 9 men in the Choking group, and 11 women and 10 men in the Control group.

Testing Plausibility

The experiment was conducted in four phases. Phase 1 was a mass-testing session, during which participants rated how plausible it was for individuals like them to have experienced each of a set of 40 events. The scale ranged from 1 (*highly implausible*) to 8 (*highly plausible*). Participants were then given a Life Events Inventory (LEI) containing 36 of the events on the plausibility scale. For each event, participants were asked to rate how certain they were that it actually had happened to them before the age of 3 (likelihood ratings). The scale ranged from 1 (*certain the event had not happened to them*) to 8 (*certain the event had happened to them*). Participants were invited to participate in the second phase of the experiment if they had given (a) low plausibility and likelihood scores (1 or 2) on the Witnessed Possession event, and (b) a high plausibility score (greater than 5) and a low likelihood score (1 or 2) on the Almost Choked event.

Phase 2, held 3 months later, presented the plausibility manipulation. This phase was skipped by participants in the control group. Participants assigned to the Possession group read 12 mini-articles about each of four different topics. Randomly placed within these 12 mini-articles were 3 articles that dealt with the topic of possession. The other 9 mini-articles concerned other topics (e.g., romantic relationships, work experiences, and the public health system). In the Choking group, participants were treated exactly like those in the Possession group, except the content of 3 of the mini-articles concerned various aspects of swallowing an object and choking. Participants in both groups were told that the purpose of the task was to assess the readability and writing style of various types of passages taken from scientific and nonscientific journals. For each article, participants evaluated how convincing and compelling it was, and how relevant it was to the topic under consideration. The articles were prepared so as to appear unconnected (i.e., taken from independent sources).

The three articles on possession were no longer than one page each. One article presented the idea that possession is quite common in the general population—especially in the Italian culture—and that witnessing possession is also common. Another article conveyed the idea that many children have witnessed possession. The article included a description of what happens in a typical possession experience (e.g., St. Vitus's dance, convulsing, falling down, foaming at the mouth, swearing, vomiting hair, and spontaneous movement of objects), and falsely conveyed the idea that adults will sometimes display symptoms of possession in front of young children under the belief that they can freely do this and the children will not remember later on. The third article contained interviews with adults describing their memories of early childhood, which included witnessing strange behaviors consistent with possession.

Phase 3 occurred 1 week after the articles had been read and contained the personalized suggestion manipulation. Like Phase 2, Phase 3 was limited to participants in the Possession and Choking groups. The experiment was conducted on an individual basis so that more personalized suggestions could be delivered. Participants completed a questionnaire about their fears. Participants in the Possession group received false feedback on the responses and were told that their fear profile was a sign that witnessing possession had probably happened to them in early childhood (before age 3). The fear profile of participants in the Choking group was interpreted as a sign that nearly choking had probably happened to them in early childhood.

Phase 4 took place 1 week after the end of Phase 3. Participants were asked to rate the plausibility of the events (the same 40 events as during the mass-testing session) and to again complete the [Life Events Inventory test] on the same subset of 36 events. . . .

The Results

Tests revealed that plausibility increased only for the implausible Witnessed Possession event after the Possession manipulation. . . . As expected, the scores for the plausible event Almost Choked were already high and did not change from pre- to posttest for any group. Together, these results demonstrate that reading the Possession mini-articles and receiving the personalized fear profile, increased the plausibility of the Witnessed Possession event.

A second purpose of the study was to assess the effect of the manipulations on confidence that the event had been personally experienced. Remember that we selected only participants who initially reported that they had not experienced the key event in early childhood. We expected an increase in confidence to occur for the event that was already plausible (Almost Choked), but we were especially interested in whether this would also occur for Witnessed Possession, the event that was initially considered implausible. . . .

Tests revealed that in the Possession group, there was a significant increase in [Life Events Inventory] scores for the Witnessed Possession event . . . and for the Almost Choked event. . . . However, the increase was significantly, greater for the Witnessed Possession event than for the Almost Choked event. . . .

In terms of [Life Events Inventory] scores, our participants initially were quite confident that witnessing possession had not happened to them in childhood (1.27 on an 8-point scale). After the Possession manipulation, the participant's mean score rose to nearly 3, still leaning on the "Didn't happen" side of the scale. It is of interest whether any of our participants moved to the "Happened" side of the scale; that is, did they move from a low score to one that was 5 or greater? We found that 18% of the participants in the Possession group gave final [Life Events Inventory] scores of 5 or greater on the Witnessed Possession event. All of them had given this event a postmanipulation plausibility rating of 3. Thus, they saw the event as relatively implausible but believed, nevertheless, that it had probably happened to them. . . .

Developing a False Belief

We found that when people were exposed to a two-part suggestion (mini-articles plus fear profile) about an already plausible event . . . they increased the perceived likelihood that the plausible event had happened to them. This result is just a replication of previous findings showing the malleability of likelihood ratings. Interestingly, we also found that the two-part suggestion on an initially implausible event, "Witnessed Possession," made participants rate this event as being less implausible and also showed increased confidence that the event happened to them in early childhood. Thus, we have demonstrated three things. First, suggestive information can increase the plausibility of an initially implausible event. Second, suggestive information can increase people's ratings of the likelihood that the event has happened to them. Third, the information can be effective not only in increasing likelihood ratings for an event that is already plausible, but also for one that is initially implausible. . . .

It is probably not too surprising that new information could make events seem less implausible. But how does that new information make some people (18% in the "Witnessed Possession" event) go from saying at one point in time that an event did not happen, to later saying that it probably did happen? When people initially state that an event did not happen, they may base this on three sources of information. First, they have no memory of the event. Second, they may not have enough knowledge about the event to realize that they may have experienced it. Third, they may have knowledge about it that allows them to reject it as part of their own autobiography.

Exposing people to new information designed to enhance plausibility removes two of the three major ways in which they know that an event did not happen to them. In these studies, participants read about possession occurring in their own culture, and they learned the "symptoms" of possession. From this, they concluded that the possibility that they had Witnessed Possession was somewhat less unlikely than they had thought. When then given false feedback indicating the likelihood that they had indeed Witnessed Possession, some of the participants concluded that they probably had witnessed it, developing in this way a false belief.

References

Barnhart, C.L. (1956). *The American college dictionary.* (New York: Random House).

Garry, M., Manning, C.G., Loftus, E.F. & Sherman, J. (1996). Imagination inflation: Imagining a childhood event inflates confidence that it occurred. *Psychonomic Bulletin & Review*, 3, 208–214.

Glucksberg, S. & McCloskey, M. (1981). Decisions about ignorance: Knowing that you don't know. *Journal of Experimental Psychology*, 311–325.

Heaps, C. & Nash, M. (1999). Individual differences in imagination inflation. *Psychonomic Bulletin & Review*, 6, 313–318.

Hunter, J.E. & Schmidt, F.L. (1990). *Methods of meta-analysis: Correcting error and bias in research findings.* (Newbury Park, CA: Sage).

Hyman, I.E., Gilstrap, L.L., Decker, K. & Wilkinson, C. (1998). Manipulating remember and know judgements of autobiographical memories. *Applied Cognitive Psychology*, 12, 371–386.

Hyman, I.E., Husband, T.H. & Billings, J.F. (1995). False memories of childhood experiences. *Applied Cognitive Psychology*, 90, 181–197.

Hyman, I.E. & Kleinknecht, E.E. (1999). False childhood memories: Research, theory, and applications.(In L.M. Williams & V.L. Banyard (Eds.), *Trauma and memory* (175–188). Thousand Oaks, CA: Sage.).

Kelley, C., Amodio, D. & Lindsay, D.S. (1996, July). *The effects of "diagnosis" and memory work on memories of handedness shaping.* (Paper presented at the International Conference on Memory, Padua, Italy.).

Koriat, A. & Liebliech, I. (1977). A study of memory pointers. *Acta Psychologica*, 41, 151–164.

Lindsay, D.S. & Read, J.D. (1994). Psychotherapy and memories of childhood sexual abuse: A cognitive perspective. *Applied Cognitive Psychology*, 8, 281–338.

Loftus, E.F. (1997, September). Creating false memories. *Scientific American*, 277, 70–75.

Lynn, S.J., Pintor, J., Stafford, J., Marmelstein, L. & Lock, T. (1998). Rendering implausible plausible: Narrative construction, suggestion, and memory. (In J. DeRivera & T.R. Sarbin (Eds.), *Believed-in imaginings: The narrative construction of reality.* Washington, DC: American Psychological Association.).

Mack, J.E. (1994). *Abduction.* (New York: Scribner).

Mazzoni, G. (in press). False memories. [Target article]. *European Psychologist.*

Mazzoni, G.A.L. & Loftus, E.F. (1998). Dreaming, believing, and remembering. (In J. DeRivera & T. R. Sarbin (Eds.), *Believed-in imaginings: The narrative construction of reality* (pp. 145–156). Washington, DC: American Psychological Association.).

Mazzoni, G.A.L., Loftus, E.F., Seitz, A. & Lynn, S.J. (1999). Changing beliefs and memories through dream interpretation. *Applied Cognitive Psychology*, 13, 125–144.

Modi v. West Virginia Board of Medicine (195 W.Va. 230, 465 S.E. 2d 230).

Olson v. Morris (1999 U.S. App. LEXIS 14681; 99 Cal. Daily Op. Service 5267; 99 Daily Journal DAR 6751).

Pezdek, K., Finger, K. & Hodge, D. (1997). Planting false childhood memories: The role of event plausibility. *Psychological Science*, 8, 437–441.

Spanos, N.P., Burgess, C.A., Burgess, M.F., Samuels, C. & Blois, W.O. (1999). Creating false memories of infancy with hypnotic and non-hypnotic procedures. *Applied Cognitive Psychology*, 13, 201–218.

Exorcism Can Harm the Mentally Ill

Bonnie Henderson Schell

Until the late nineteenth century, it was a commonly held belief that mental disorders were the work of demons. Even today, some graduate-level seminary programs in pastoral counseling teach that mental illness is a symptom of demonic influence and should be dealt with as a spiritual problem.

To Bonnie Henderson Schell, director of the Mental Health Client Action Network in Santa Cruz, California, contemporary belief in demonic possession represents one more attempt to intrude on the dignity and autonomy of those who suffer from mental illness. Schell argues that exorcism places too much power in the hands of manipulative spiritual leaders, interfering with the victim's ability to assess his or her own psychological needs.

And as [Jesus] stepped out on land, there met him a man from the city who had demons; for a long time he had worn

Bonnie Henderson Schell, "'I Beg You, Do Not Torment Me,'" *The Humanist*, May/June 1992. Copyright © 1992 by *The Humanist*. Reproduced by permission.

no clothes, and he lived not in a house but among the tombs. When he saw Jesus, he fell down before him and cried, "What have you to do with me, Jesus . . . ? I beg you, do not torment me." For he had commanded the unclean spirit to come out of the man. . . . Luke 8:27–29

On April 5, 1991, the television news show *20/20* broadcast the now-infamous "exorcism" of a 16-year-old girl named Gina. Nearly a year later, the images of that media atrocity still haunt me. As someone who was also diagnosed schizophrenic as a teenager, I watched the *20/20* exorcism with anger, fear, and envy. *Anger* that my own internal confusion and despair were now going to be treated as possession by some *external* power, after I had spent years learning to be responsible for my emotional turmoil and to cope with my cognitive difference. *Fear* that television was going to deceive the public by representing Gina's suffering as part of the cosmic battle between good and evil—surely the basis of all spectacle—with the sick and the insane mere bit players.

And *envy*, tangible, aching envy—the reaction most shared by other ex-mental patients who watched with me. When *they* had been "actively psychotic," as Gina was described, friends and family shunned them, ward nurses stuck them in seclusion without water or toilets, and they were lucky to have any talk therapy longer than 15 minutes twice a month. Yet here was a psychotherapist, a nurse, a translator, the exorcist, a medical doctor, and several others all intent on freeing Gina from her burden.

I visited a United Methodist Church in Santa Cruz on April 7, two days after the exorcism was broadcast, assuming it would be a topic of discussion. It was not. The congregation sang, "Silence, frenzied, unclean spirit." I looked to see how ancient this obscure hymn might be, only to find that the words were written in 1984 by Thomas Troeger.

Deliverance Ministry

That evening, I was talking with Kimsey, a 55-year-old veteran who considers himself a survivor of mental-health hospitals. I naively remarked that Protestants would never stage the kind of stunt the Catholics had pulled off on TV. "Where have you been?" Kimsey asked. "Don't you know about the Deliverance Meetings on the outskirts of town?" I didn't, but Kimsey did. He had visited an independent evangelical church one Sunday wearing his "Psychiatric Survivor" button. That evening, four persons appeared at his door and insisted that he accompany them to a meeting. There, he was held down and banged on the forehead with a heavy redwood cross until he figured out what he was expected to say; he quickly renounced Satan, praised Jesus, and asked to be taken back to his apartment to pray. No member of the congregation subsequently called to check on Kimsey, to invite him to church, or, for that matter, to see how he was getting along on his disability income.

A few days later, I sought out an anthropology professor at the University of California at Santa Cruz whose special interest is studying the discourse of Jerry Falwell. I again spouted off about not believing that a ritual from 1614 was being used in 1991 by people in their right minds (more or less). She simply smiled at me. Did she know any good research on the topic I might read? Yes, she said, but I didn't need the library; all I had to do was go to the local grocery store and look for the *Darkness* books by Frank E. Peretti.

"Under Attack from a Global Occult Conspiracy"

Peretti is a former associate pastor at an Assemblies of God church and the author of "Dungeons & Dragons"-type adventures for teens. His novels, *This Present Darkness* (1986) and *Piercing the Darkness* (1989), depict a world of relentless spiritual warfare, where God's guerrilla warriors (all male angels)—the protectors of small towns and Christian schools like the Good Shepherd Academy—do battle with the organized spirits of darkness called Deception, Hatred, Violence, Divination, Despair, Fear, Ba-al, Strongman, and Insanity. In Peretti's novels, Christians are under attack by a global occult conspiracy and its malevolent mind-control campaign. Even a school curriculum entitled "Finding the Real Me—Self-Esteem and Personal Fulfillment Studies for Fourth Graders" emanates satanic vibrations.

The *Darkness* narratives held the top two spots on Christian bestseller lists for more than a year. (*Piercing the Darkness* is still number four in 1992 and already in its sixth printing.) More ominously, Peretti's books have moved to the bestseller lists in general independent and chain stores, and Howard (*Raiders of the Lost Ark*) Kazahjian has bought the film rights to both.

Perhaps not surprisingly, publishers are rushing to provide Christian readers with books reinforcing their notions of a world turned morally upside down due to demonic intervention. In February 1991, Moody Press issued Merrill Unger's *What Demons Can Do to Saints*. John Knox Press issued *Overcoming Depression* by Paul Hauck, which has already sold over 50,000 copies. The *Christian Care Books* and *Guides for Productive Living* are edited by Wayne Oates, a professor of psychiatry and behavioral science at the University of Louisville School of Medicine and a professor at Southern Baptist Theological Seminary. And worldwide comprehensive mental-health care, biblically based, is offered by Drs. Frank Minirth and Paul Meier, both psychiatrists with over 30 self-help books to their credit, as well as one-week care clinics in 19 cities, a nationwide radio and television program, a video home-counseling library, and a slick new quarterly, *Today's Better Life*.

Demons and Mental Illness

These new books from Christian presses, together with the 20/20 exorcism, represent a troubling resurgence of the eighteenth-century evangelical model of treating mental illness. In the 1700s, mental afflictions were exclusively the province of the clergy. Cotton Mather, a learned man in Latin and medicine as well as a gifted preacher, lamented the "melancholy indispositions" of a good many pious New Englanders which prevented their continuing in useful service to the Commonwealth of Massachusetts. Mather believed these spells, as well as his third wife's "distraction," to be ordained by God to test the Christian's patience and resolve. Entire congregations prayed at the bedsides of those stricken with melancholy. In "Insaniabilia: An Essay upon Incurables," Mather argued that sin was the root cause of mental illness and that "some devils" (only with God's permission) might take advantage of moral weakness to destroy the body politic.

The evangelical model, however, gave way in the nineteenth century to the moral model, largely based on the work of the French doctor Phillippe Pinel, who prescribed kindness, routine, work, and the disciplining of folly. By this view, sickness was seen as the result of excess—of reading, emotions, will, bad habits, or nervous fibers—and moderation was recommended in all things.

The first two public hospitals built to test the moral model in Massachusetts were run by white Protestant superintendents with high ideals to resocialize the insane. When, however, immigrants admitted to the asylums after 1840 did not respond to a different culture's ideas for right living designed to "restore" their reason and correct their behavior, the superintendents faced mounting statistics of failure. The problem was addressed by building more public asylums for the paupers and the foreign-born and sedating the unruly with strong doses of opium.

In 1825, the Superior Court of Massachusetts presciently acknowledged a shift to the medical model when it stopped referring to madness as "that most calamitous visitation from Providence" and substituted the word *disease*. The medical model conceives of mental illness as a disease which is physiologically based, with symptoms that are manifestations of organic dysfunction (even though the precise explanation for how this occurs may not be known). Thus, general practitioners graduating from the first medical colleges took responsibility for the insane away from the ministers; witchcraft, for example, became *infectious mania*. The supremacy of the medical model was further ensured in 1917 when a syphilitic infection was positively identified as the cause of general paralysis, previously thought to be insanity because those with the venereal disease had impaired judgment, difficulty concentrating, memory loss, disregard for appearance, and muscular weakness.

The Alternative to Exorcism

For the past 30 years, however, the medical model has itself been the subject of attack. Critics of the medical model have collectively charged that its treatments are ineffective, that mental illness has not been scientifically shown to be a disease, and that psychiatry has gained too much institutional power.

Moreover, the medical model of insanity is reductionist. It assumes that neural pathways, rather than content, account completely for the organization of memory, sense, learning, consciousness, and problem-solving—irrespective of social and political variables. This reductionism constructs a particular view of the person as made up of various biological parts to be managed by electroshock, sedation, MAO inhibitors, neuroleptics, seclusion, and restraints. This is a selective view, but because of psychiatry's "scientific" status, it is the prevailing one.

Three million persons in the United States—and lately the number has been inflated to one family in five—have been identified by institutional psychiatry as being afflicted with severe mental disorders. The well-being and safety of those so identified are, regrettably, not the concern of psychiatry in its self-adjudicated power to dispense medications. Side effects reported by researchers are called *disadvantages*—even liver failure. Daily stupor and diarrhea are merely "unpleasant." Patients are labeled "perpetual whiners," incompetent to speak about their own bodies or to reject treatments which they find dehumanizing, punitive, and antitherapeutic. Except for Deliverance Ministry itself, there is no better example than psychiatry in which power relations distort practice so profoundly. . . .

Ironically, the institutional power of psychiatry, the top position of drug companies in the Fortune 500, even Scientology's attempts to provide the victims of psychiatric medication with forums on national talk shows (while setting up its own alternative psychiatric hospitals) have all arguably prodded the old evangelical model into renewed life.

Deliverance and Its Theology

Today's evangelical model, however, flounders on its new absurdities. Professing Christians, for instance, are not subject to scrutiny since, if they are filled with the Holy Spirit, they cannot be host to an evil presence at the same time. In *Demonism: How to Win Against the Devil*, Charles Swindoll hedges his bets by arguing that Satan does not choose persons with schizophrenia or other serious psychotic disorders because he needs intact, well-functioning persons to accomplish his ends.

So, who, according to today's Deliverance Ministry, is at

risk of demonic possession? Interestingly, just as psychiatry once pinned the blame for schizophrenic children on "controlling mothers" and "passive fathers," the evangelical model explains a child's bond to Satan by the occult practices of relatives dating back at least four centuries. In his *Believer's Guide to Spiritual Warfare*, Thomas White advises parents to look for spirits "that gained entrance into the bloodline" as evidenced by relatives who have committed suicide or who have a history of depression or psychiatric illnesses. Such is Deliverance Ministry's fear of the anxiety and uncertainty which inevitably accompany freedom of thought that, according to White, feeling anxious or uncertain may mean you are the target of demon possession.

C. Fred Dickason, in *Demon Possession and the Christian*, attempts to steer the troubled Christian away from the competition by warning that the Angel of Light can appear as a false teacher or a false counselor. Satan corrupts music, art, books, medications, possessions, status, and relationships—thus placing choice in all of these areas under the jurisdiction of the Deliverance Minister. The evangelical model of curing mental illness has even taken a leaf from New Age neo-paganism, which defines evil as that which inhibits the actualization of one's full potential. Savvy language practitioners of the evangelical model have begun to substitute *evil oppression* for *demonic possession.*

"Mere Suspicion or Malice"

In *Demonism: How to Win Against the Devil*, Charles Swindoll lists the following as indicators of demonic possession: sudden and unreasonable changes of mood; aggressive, unrestrainable expressions of hostility; extreme, enslaving habits of sexual immorality, perversion, or gross blasphemy; and unnatural attachment to charms, fortune-telling, and involvement in the occult. In *Counseling and the*

Demonic (1988), Rodger Bufford provides these clues to identifying demonic possession: "resistance to benefits from medication and psychotherapy"; "negative reactions . . . to Christian religious practices"; and a "history of living in areas without a strong Judeo-Christian cultural influence." Needless to say, these vague and expansive lists are wide open to interpretive abuse—as has been the case historically. In "An Account of the Imprisonment and Sufferings of Robert Fuller of Cambridge," published in Boston in 1833, Fuller expressed his misgivings about the increase in the number of the insane once institutions for them were erected. "Mere suspicion or malice," he observed, "is enough to fix on anyone the charge of insanity."

Charges of demonic possession have traditionally increased once people start to look for it; to persons who only understand hammers, everything looks like a nail. Thus, in *Counseling and the Demonic*, Bufford advises Christians to look for demonic possession among "American Indian and Oriental ethnic groups." He goes on to observe that "missionaries and foreign nationals report that they are much more able to spot evidence of satanic activity in unfamiliar cultures than in their own," and concludes that, "in the sense that all evil is the result of sin in the world, mental disorders are the result of sin." Of course, it is ridiculous to place mental disorders in the same category with such things as the savings-and-loan scandal, the starvation of children, death squads, political corruption, and the many other serious evils in our world and label them all as "the result of sin."

Even the Reverend James LeBar, an exorcism consultant, had to implicitly concede this point. When asked by Ted Koppel in the followup on *Nightline* to the *20/20* exorcism why he thought the devil would pick a young woman to persecute, LeBar hypothesized that her possession served as the devil's "distraction" from the big evils—hunger, abortion, divorce, and so on. (I wonder if the bright lights prevented Koppel from seriously considering his own role in this distraction. Where LeBar, Swindoll et. al would undoubtedly recognize the mark of satanic conspiracy, others might see a stupefied public that has surrendered its cognitive agenda to a sensationalistic and profit-driven media.) In any event, if the church is easily sidetracked, it is not by Satan but by its own panic over the loss of its effectiveness in society.

The theory of demonic possession puts Christian psychologists in a compromising position. For instance, if Gina's exorcist, Father A., went to a psychiatrist who was a religious skeptic and confided that he felt called to confront the minions of Satan, that he believed physical bodies could be possessed by the invisible spirit of evil, and that he was afraid of feeling too much compassion for the victim, Father A. would be diagnosed as a 295.3 [paranoid schizophrenic] in the *Diagnostic and Statistical Manual III*. The prognosis would not be good, especially if he was also pacing the floor all night in his search for an answer to his theological dilemma. Some Christians seem barely to recognize this contradiction; an employment ad for a Christian psychologist in *Christianity Today* (April 29, 1991) promises "unique opportunity, spiritual warfare, and excitement guaranteed!" Others, like John MacArthur in *Our Sufficiency in Christ* (1991), maintain that the church's embrace of psychology is Satan's greatest coup. And Martin and Deidre Bobgan's position is clear from the title of their 1987 book, *Psychoheresy: The Psychological Seduction of Christianity.*

Psychiatry Versus Deliverance Ministry

Historically, attempts to impose order and control over the deviant are a compensation for swift and staggering change in the social order. Neither psychiatry nor Christianity are exempt from acting as agents of social control. Whether through compromise or competition, Christianity is attempting to wrest from psychiatry control over the body and mind. . . .

Both Christianity and institutional psychiatry want to practice a Deliverance Ministry which takes as its object persons already denied self-determination—already disabled rather than enabled by the mental-health system, which has a vested interest in a chronic clientele and its own megagrowth.

Neither fundamentalist Christianity nor institutional psychiatry has much tolerance or respect for individual differences, for "odd-balls," or for troublemakers who persist in questioning its motives and ethical practices. Thus, many Deliverance Ministers and mental-health-system providers enter other peoples' lives of suffering not as healers but as authorities claiming to know what is in someone else's best interest, and they each claim the power to impose solutions on another's body and mind. . . .

The *object* of research and medication, incarceration and dispossession, needs to be recognized as the *subject* that he or she truly is. That subject continues to plead, "I beg you, do not torment me."

We cannot allow Deliverance Ministry to set itself up as the conscience of the mental-health-care system. Instead, we must insist to those who want to impose the evangelical model on the one hand and the medical model on the other that well-being is not only psychological or biological but social, intellectual, and political. Ultimately, we must hold both Christianity and the mental-health-care system to the Hippocratic oath to "do no harm or injustice" in their attempts to cure.

Exorcism Can Be Dangerous

David James Smith

Many forms of exorcism are both emotionally charged and intensely physical, and some overzealous exorcists have accidentally killed their patients. In a few documented cases, violent people have even used exorcism as an excuse to inflict "legitimate" physical injury on others. Even when no physical assault takes place, exorcism can cause psychological damage—particularly if the allegedly demon-possessed individual already suffers from an undiagnosed, reality-distorting mental illness.

In this article, true crime writer and *Sunday Times* journalist David James Smith discusses the physical and mental dangers of undergoing an exorcism. His article centers on the story of "Mary," a government clerk whose life became dramatically worse after her exorcism. Smith argues that exorcism—even when it consists of rare sessions, and does not involve obvious physical or emotional trauma—can cause long-term damage to some patients.

She was 47 years old and could barely talk. She could speak fluently in tongues, but intelligible words stuck in her throat and stuttered from her lips. It had been worse on the phone. You could tell it was her because there was nobody there, just a faint, quickened breathing. It took five minutes or so for her to speak her address.

She lived alone in a small, neat flat on an estate in the suburbs of a northern city. Children played outside and dogs were barking. There was a Bible on the dining table, a hand's reach from where she sat. A video cassette lay on the video recorder beneath the television: the film about that singing nun, *The Sound of Music*.

Her hands twisted and curled at the wrists, her head made frantic, jerky movements and her eyes darted everywhere to avoid contact. "I'm very nervous," she managed to say. She wanted to talk, especially now that she felt so much better, but she was torn between declaring herself, revealing her identity in this article, and her fear of the consequences. We agreed that she would be called Mary.

It had been terrible when Mary still believed whatever she was told. She was told she was possessed by demons. Lots of demons. Whole families of them. They had names and everything. She had felt that they were controlling her. They had taken over her body and her life. They needed to be cast out. She had wanted deliverance.

Someone at her church had said she should go to Ellel Grange. They specialised in that sort of thing. She had dreamt about going there and took it to be a good sign. She had been very happy on her way to Ellel Grange. She had felt she was going to the top place, the Harley Street of deliverance ministry. They had given her a cup of tea when she arrived and made her feel very welcome. She thought she had found the answer to all her problems.

The Deliverance Movement

How do you begin to explain the renewal of interest in the devil, demons and exorcism? Here is an ancient idea that people who did bad things, or even just different things, had embraced or been invaded by external forces of evil. Back then, people were ostracised, persecuted, condemned as witches, burnt or otherwise disposed of.

Supposedly we are wiser now. Psychology and psychiatry indicate that the roots of "aberrant" behaviour are within us. They emerge from family experience, trauma, all kinds of abuse, organic illness. . . . These often complex ideas demand patience and hard work to overcome and tolerance to understand. How much easier, safer and less threatening to dismiss the child-killer among us as the embodiment of evil, or the torment inside us as the devil's work, from which we can be delivered.

Mary's quest for deliverance had taken her to a booming outpost of that phenomenon of Christian revival, the charismatic renewal. The enthusiasm for demons and deliverance among some charismatics is causing concern in the mainstream churches. Strictly speaking, in its original meaning, "charisma" is a spiritual power handed down by God. As described in the Bible, these powers are the gift of the Holy Spirit—the ability to speak in tongues, to heal by the laying-on of hands, to prophesy, to discern demons and to deliver those who have succumbed to the devil. As its name implies, the charismatic renewal has rediscovered the use of these gifts. As a movement it has spread rapidly across all boundaries of Christianity over the past 25 years. You could call it evangelical, or back-to-basics, or Christian fundamentalism.

It is said that there are more than 30 [million] Catholic

charismatics around the world and even more Protestants, including a strong charismatic element within the Church of England. Outside the mainstream churches, the movement has spawned many new independent groups—they are often called house churches—and evengelical ministries such as the Ellel Ministries, whose headquarters, Ellel Grange, is in Lancashire. Ellel Ministries was founded in 1986 by an Oxford chemistry graduate and former lecturer, Peter Horrobin. It now has two further centres in the south of England, as well as bases in Canada and eastern Europe. It has an annual turnover in excess of £1m.

The charismatic movement has breathed new life into the Christian churches, and there is a sense that, depending on your point of view, it has captured, or exploited, the mood of the times. Certainly, the renewal has polarised contemporary theological thinking about the devil. The renewed belief in the healing powers of God has inevitably reawakened belief in the powers of darkness. Charismatics often see themselves on the front line of a spiritual battle between good and evil. More moderate and modern theologians, who thought the church had moved on from that battle, worry about the dangers of "demonising".

Both the Roman Catholic and Anglican Churches have structures in place to control the application of deliverance ministry. Each diocese is supposed to have someone—the Catholics still call them exorcists, the Church of England likes to talk of "advisers"—who deals with such cases. The diocesan bishop must give permission before an exorcism is carried out. Outside the mainstream, among the house churches and the independent ministries, there is little or no control.

Mary's Story

Mary did not know where her problems had begun, only that they were caused by demons. Her parents had been dominating and undermining. She had begun to stutter while she was still at school. At college she had been involved in a degrading sexual experience with two men. She could not say it was rape exactly because, ever compliant, she felt she had gone along with it.

Then she had become the most faithful and financially supportive member of a small city church, which she had come to recognise as a cult. She had been totally subservient to the church code, not cutting her hair because she was told not to, never wearing trousers, fasting one day a week, praying for three hours a day and going regularly to the main city square to preach—her, with her speech difficulty, preaching. It had been a torment. Slowly she had lost all sense of herself. It had taken her 12 years to leave the cult church.

She had joined a Pentecostal church and a pastor had begun counselling her. He knew all about the cult and the bad sexual experience. The men involved had been African. He told her she had a voodoo spirit inside her and was in need of deliverance. The pastor called in a friend who was a deliverance minister. She could not remember much about that. She recalled falling on the floor, clutching at the legs of her minister, believing the demon was leaving her. The effect did not last long. She changed pastors and began to be counselled by a couple in the same church. They, too, discerned demons and began deliverance. She fell off a chair and tried to get out of the door, almost fighting the couple to escape. She could only think it was anger that was driving her.

The couple thought they were witnessing the manifestation of a very powerful demon. Too powerful for them to cast out. She had better go to Ellel Grange. She contacted Ellel Ministries and was invited to the grange for a weekend healing retreat.

The Exorcism

It seemed very nice there. The cup of tea, the loving welcome, the relaxing atmosphere of the place, which was an old country estate near Lancaster, set in many acres of grounds. She was surprised, though, that there was not more counselling from the counsellors. They seemed to be working from a questionnaire or a check list of demons. Have you ever been sexually abused? and that sort of thing. She had never had her palm read or looked at horoscopes or been into the occult, so they could not be her demons, even though they were on the list. She had demons of her own. She told them about the cult and about her bad sexual experience.

After a day's teaching about Jesus and the healing ministry, there was a prayer service on the Saturday evening. There was a counsellor alongside her, saying things like, "Spirit, you've got no right to be inside this child of God, you've got no right to be here, and right now, on the authority of the name of Jesus, I command this demon to leave, now. . . now. . . now go." She noticed that the counsellor found some of the demons a bit stubborn. The counsellor would say, "This is a bit stubborn, just relax, let it go." She started screaming almost immediately. Then someone else in the room began screaming too. The counsellor asked her to stop screaming because it was her demon interacting with the other person's demon.

That first weekend was a start, but she felt a little disappointed because there was obviously a long way to go. She went back to Ellel Grange three or four times. She was told she had many demons. There were so many, she could barely remember what they were called, but they all had names. She had demons from each of the three main families. There was a control spirit, the Jezebel spirit, the monkey spirit, more animal spirits, the spirit that had entered her from her dead grandmother. . . .

On her final visit she felt she was ready for the main deliverance. She was taken into a room on her own with two counsellors. The friend who had given her a lift to Ellel Grange was waiting outside in the car park for three hours. Mary was inside, writhing on the floor, screaming, coughing, crying, retching as the counsellors prayed and cast out her multitude of demons. Eventually they stopped and said something like, "Well, we've been praying for a long time now and a lot's been done; we've had a good session today, shall we leave it for now?" They said there was only a little bit further to go. She was exhausted from all the drama. She told the counsellors she hoped it wasn't just her putting on a big act. They reassured her that they didn't think she could be as dramatic as that. She felt relieved and happy and sang joyous hymns all the way home in the car. She thought she was free at last.

Surrounded by Evil Spirits

As part of the aftercare assistance, she left Ellel Grange with a leaflet that advised her, among other things, to put on the full armour of God every morning. This came from a biblical reference from Ephesians: the belt of truth, the breastplate of righteousness, feet fitted with the readiness that comes from the gospel of peace, the shield of faith, the helmet of salvation, the sword of the Spirit. She acted this out every morning for a while.

It wasn't long before the "little bit" left over from her last session began to nag away at her. It became a bigger bit and bigger still. She became newly obsessed with demonic possession and felt terribly let down by Ellel Grange. She became paranoid. Having been taught that coughing and sneezing were demonic manifestations, she began to believe her own coughs and sneezes were demons and that everyone else's were too. She noticed the dogs outside her window started barking when she prayed. She thought they were also evil spirits.

It seemed that the atmosphere changed whenever she went into a room. She believed it was her demons influencing everybody there. When people sighed or said they were fed up, she felt it was her demons. She was conscious of the demons inside her every minute of the day. She felt she was in hell. Somehow, over all these years, she had maintained a job as a local government clerk. Now she began taking more and more time off sick. She was depressed and wondered if she had a split personality, which she misdiagnosed as schizophrenia. She began to consider admitting herself to a psychiatric hospital. When she told her church pastors, they were disapproving. If you choose to go that way, you're choosing the way of the world rather than the way of God, they told her. She was trapped.

Her experiences in the cult church began reappearing to her as nightmares. After one particularly unpleasant flashback dream she went into work one morning and could not stop crying. She hid in the toilets until a colleague came to find her. It was not the first time this had happened. Again she went to see her welfare officers. She'd been seeing them regularly but never really listened, because the welfare officers were atheists. Now the senior welfare officer began phoning round the country, trying to find someone who could help. It was funny how, in the end, Mary's help really did come through the way of the world and not through an exorcist. . . .

Obsessed No Longer

The welfare officer, the way of the world, had been Mary's bridge back to reality. By chance, the officer had contacted a psychiatrist who knew a former Pentecostal preacher, Graham Baldwin, who helped people who had been involved in cults and bad religion through his organisation, Catalyst. He, too, had dealt with Ellel casualties.

She told him about the coughs and sneezes, her own and everyone else's, that plagued her. She told him they were demons. She sneezed. He reached out and snatched at the air. "Caught one," he said. She laughed. "Yes, it is ridiculous, isn't it?" he said. It was the beginning of her recovery. Her own private renewal.

He tried to count all the demons she had been told she possessed, or was possessed by. He stopped at 46. He got out the Bible and tried to help her see that Jezebel and many of the others were not really demon spirits.

When she went back to work, her welfare officer could not believe the change. The stutter was still there but better. The anxiety and the lack of self-esteem were still there but better. She was still a very sad woman with a very sad past, who was in need of help. But she was no longer infested with demons.

Epilogue: Analyzing the Evidence

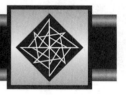

Each article in this book makes an argument for or against the existence of demonic possession and the usefulness of exorcism rituals. Because these issues can have strong religious implications, people tend to hold passionate beliefs about them. Someone who accepts the existence of demonic possession as an article of faith would understandably have a different perspective than someone whose religious beliefs specifically exclude the possibility of demonic possession.

This epilogue will draw no conclusions about demonic possession and exorcism; instead, it will provide a time-tested method that you can use to evaluate arguments such as those included in this book.

About the Author

One of the first things to do when evaluating an argument is to examine the author's background and qualifications. Although an author's credentials and biases do not determine the quality of an argument, they can offer insight into how credible and well researched an author's data is likely to be. Has the author any special qualifications for writing about the subject? Is the author a respected writer known for accurate research? Does the author have any noticeable biases? The answers to these questions may give you a preliminary idea of the sort of argument you might encounter.

The Five-Step Approach

When an author presents an argument, he or she is essentially making a case; when you respond to that argument, you are essentially rendering a verdict. In a courtroom, juries are asked to consider the claim and the evidence, then reach a verdict based on the merits of the case. This process—also used by scientists and many philosophers—is called hypothetical reasoning. Although the term is used by different people in different ways, it involves a common five-step process:

1. State the author's hypothesis (claim).
2. Gather the author's supporting evidence.
3. Examine the author's supporting evidence.
4. Consider alternative hypotheses (claims).
5. Draw your own conclusion about the author's argument.

If this sounds too easy, remember that hypothetical reasoning is a way of evaluating specific claims, not a shortcut to certainty. You are always welcome to suspend judgment on issues discussed in this book if you have not made up your mind about them.

In the sections below, we will use hypothetical reasoning to evaluate two articles from this book. You can practice applying the method to as many of the other articles as you like.

1. State the Author's Hypothesis

A hypothesis is a testable statement. For example, if you leave an ice cube on the table and return an hour later to find a small puddle in its place, you might hypothesize that the ice cube melted. Someone else might hypothesize that the ice cube was taken off the table by someone with wet hands. Most articles in this book make one or more claims about demonic possessions and exorcism. Each article's title describes its main point. The following table shows some of the articles' main points restated as hypotheses:

Author	Hypothesis
Joe Beam	Demons can possess human beings.
Roy Clements	Demonic possession is best understood not as a symptom of mental illness but as a meaningful diagnosis that may have both psychological and religious components.
M. Scott Peck	Exorcism can heal people.
Francis MacNutt	
Michael W. Cuneo	Belief in demonic possession can be attributed primarily to sociological factors.
Giuliana A.L. Mazzoni, Elizabeth F. Loftus, and Irving Kirsch	
Bonnie Henderson Schell	Exorcism treats the mentally ill in a degrading and inhumane way.
David James Smith	

A good hypothesis is always clear, specific, and provable:

1. *Clear.* The meaning of the hypothesis should be relatively obvious and stated in a concise way.
2. *Specific.* The hypothesis should be a specific claim, not a general one. For example, "Exorcism is real" is too broad and vague. "Exorcism expels real evil spirits" is more tangible. In cases where the argument itself is necessarily vague—for example, if the author is arguing that exorcism is beneficial but is unsure why—then the vagueness itself should be mentioned as part of the hypothesis ("Exorcism is a real phenomenon, but the reasons for its success are unclear").
3. *Provable (and disprovable).* It should be possible, at least in theory, to prove or disprove any hypothesis based on evidence. A hypothesis should state alleged fact,

not pure opinion (though it can state an alleged fact about pure opinion, such as, "Most Americans believe that the Devil exists").

Three other articles in the table above do not have hypotheses listed. After reading the articles, try to translate each article's most important argument into a clear, specific, and provable hypothesis.

M. Scott Peck: "Exorcism Can Heal People"

Now that we have examined the authors' hypotheses, let's apply the hypothetical reasoning process to one of them. Here we will discuss M. Scott Peck's article, beginning on page 45.

2. Gather the Author's Supporting Evidence

After determining what the author's case is, we can take a look at how he or she intends to support it. For our purposes, the term *evidence* includes any idea or fact that the author uses to support a claim. Here are six pieces of evidence that Peck uses to support his hypothesis that exorcism is a serious and worthwhile form of therapy:

1. Peck, a trained psychiatrist, has come to believe that demonic possession is real.
2. Peck claims to have witnessed two successful exorcisms.
3. Peck claims that religious rituals such as exorcism have a psychotherapeutic role in helping people heal.
4. In the ritual of exorcism, a healer or practitioner invokes the power of God to heal the possessed.
5. Exorcism is radical and dangerous; however, many radical and dangerous medical procedures are generally considered worthwhile.
6. Peck claims that the exorcisms he witnessed probably saved the patients' lives.

3. Examine the Author's Supporting Evidence

Peck's argument relies heavily on his credibility as a psychiatrist and author. Here we will discuss three types of evidence used by Peck: opinions and testimonials, eyewitness testimony, and statements of fact.

Opinions and expert testimonials (items 1, 3, and 6). Opinions tend to be among the weakest kind of evidence, but they can be convincing under certain circumstances. When an opinion is provided by an unbiased expert, it is referred to as an expert opinion, or testimonial. In a court of law, an expert witness—an unbiased individual who is particularly well versed in a given field—may be called upon to support or denounce a claim based on his or her credentials, experience, and reputation.

It is possible to weigh an opinion or testimonial using three steps:

1. *Determine the authority's credentials.* An opinion or testimonial is strongest when the source is better qualified to render an opinion on the subject than most of his or her audience. Most of us would accept whatever Stephen Hawking has to say about particle physics because he is regarded as an expert in the field, but we would be less likely to believe what a stand-up comedian has to say about the subject.

2. *Check for bias.* No matter what an expert's credentials may be, any hint of bias can call an opinion or testimonial into question. The president of a fast-food chain may indeed know far more than most of us do about hamburgers, but we would be justifiably skeptical about any statements he or she made about the nutritional value of red meat.

3. *Whenever possible, double-check a quoted opinion or testimonial.* Sometimes credible authority figures are (in-

tentionally or unintentionally) quoted out of context to strengthen an argument. It is useful to know whether they really mean to say what they are quoted as saying.

Most of Peck's argument relies on his experience as a psychiatrist. Although Peck acknowledges that his argument does not constitute ironclad proof in favor of the efficacy of exorcism, his credentials do carry some weight. On the other hand, the fact that he is the author of a book on the efficacy of exorcism suggests that he is biased in his belief about this subject.

What do you think? Does his background as a psychiatrist make for a convincing personal testimony in favor of the efficacy of exorcism?

Eyewitness testimony (item 2). Eyewitness testimony plays a significant role in human life, and its importance is difficult to overstate. We receive information on current events based on eyewitness testimony from journalists, and historians base much of their knowledge of the ancient world on recorded eyewitness testimony.

The drawback to eyewitness testimony is that it is the easiest kind of evidence to fabricate. Anyone can instantly generate a piece of eyewitness testimony by lying, and even honest eyewitnesses can be fooled, make an honest mistake, hallucinate, or remember incorrectly. Here are two factors worth considering when you find yourself presented with eyewitness testimony:

1. *The credibility of the witness.* Does the witness have a track record of dishonest or unreliable behavior? Alternately, does the witness have a track record of honest or reliable behavior? Does the witness stand to gain—or lose—anything by coming forward? What are the witness's relevant credentials? Was the witness intoxicated or under unusual personal stress at the

time of the event (or testimony)? Could the witness be biased?

2. *The credibility of the testimony.* Can the testimony be corroborated by other eyewitness testimony or other forms of evidence? Alternately, is the testimony contradicted by other eyewitness testimony or other forms of evidence? Does it contradict itself? When the testimony is meant to describe a specific event, was it recorded soon after the event—reducing the chances that the witness's memory has become hazy over time?

Peck's argument is couched in his experiences with two exorcism patients. He does not describe his experiences in any great depth (and, as a psychiatrist, may feel that he is bound not to do so out of respect for his patients' privacy). However, he does clearly indicate that he believes he witnessed real demonic possession and real exorcisms in these two cases and that the resulting exorcisms were necessary.

What do you think? After reading the article and considering the information provided in this section, do you find Peck's eyewitness testimony to be credible?

Statements of fact (item 5). A statement of fact is a verifiable claim that something is true. For example, "I saw a dog in the hallway" is an example of eyewitness testimony, but "there was a dog in the hallway" is a statement of fact. Statements of fact can be as complex and dubious as the claims they are used to support, or they can represent established principles and historical facts that can be easily verified using everyday reference materials. When you are confronted with a statement of fact that cannot be easily verified, it is usually helpful to mentally apply the same five-step hypothetical reasoning process to it that you would apply to larger arguments.

Peck's claim that exorcism calls on God's help can be easily confirmed by checking various rites of exorcism. Jewish,

Christian, and Islamic exorcism traditions all invoke God directly, but some nonmonotheistic traditions call on a lesser deity, a human, or even other evil forces. Whether Peck's statement of fact is true depends primarily on what one supposes his context to be. If he is referring to exorcism as it is generally carried out in the Western religious traditions, his claim is verifiable.

4. Consider Alternative Hypotheses

The next step in examining a hypothesis is to see how it addresses alternative explanations for the evidence. Many authors fail to represent competing theories, or they represent them in an unfair and incomplete way. Although a one-sided argument is not necessarily a sign that the hypothesis is false, it is usually a sign that the author has not done a thorough job of supporting his or her claim.

The author's tone is sometimes a good indicator of how well he or she addresses alternative hypotheses. Does the author give the alternative hypotheses a reasonable amount of consideration and respect? If the author's tone seems patronizing or inappropriately hostile, he or she may not be considering the alternative hypotheses on a rational level. Furthermore, an author who describes an alternative hypothesis in such a way that it seems obviously unbelievable is not giving fair consideration to competing arguments about a phenomenon.

Peck's article seldom addresses alternative hypotheses directly, but it acknowledges that they are compelling and expresses a certain amount of respect for them.

5. Draw Your Own Conclusion

After studying the evidence and considering any other objections or concerns that you might have, you are in a position to evaluate the strength of the author's argument using hypothetical reasoning. It is usually possible to classify your judgment of an author's argument into one of the following five categories. Please note that this scale measures how much you agree with an author's argument, not how much you agree with an author's conclusion. Good arguments can be made on behalf of bad ideas, and vice versa.

1. *Acceptance.* You find the author's argument to be extremely convincing. All of its major points are credible, and it has no substantial flaws.
2. *Limited acceptance.* You find the author's argument to be somewhat convincing, but it has noticeable flaws.
3. *Neutrality.* You are not ready to judge the author's argument. Perhaps it assumes knowledge in fields you are not familiar with or deals entirely with abstract arguments that you do not feel qualified to evaluate.
4. *Limited disagreement.* The author's argument is fairly weak but contains enough merit to justify further discussion.
5. *Dismissal.* The author's argument completely falls apart under criticism. All important evidence is either unconvincing or misrepresented.

How would you rank M. Scott Peck's argument? What are its strongest points? What are its weakest points? How would you improve it?

Michael W. Cuneo: "Demonic Possession Cases Can Be Explained by Cultural Factors"

Before we begin the practical exercises, let's examine another article. Read Michael W. Cuneo's piece, "Demonic Possession Cases Can Be Explained by Cultural Factors," on page 66.

1. State the Author's Hypothesis

The belief in demonic possession can be attributed primarily to sociological factors.

2. Gather the Author's Supporting Evidence

1. Demonic possession became a popular idea during the 1970s.
2. Cuneo attributes the growth of the belief in demonic possession in the 1970s to the widespread success of William Peter Blatty's *The Exorcist* and Malachi Martin's book *Hostage to the Devil.*
3. Cuneo argues that those who claim to be demonically possessed will often feel obligated to mimic possession symptoms during exorcism that they have seen represented in books and movies.
4. Cuneo has witnessed more than fifty exorcisms and has seen nothing that he does not regard as the work of human beings.
5. Cuneo argues that exorcism's positive results can be attributed to the placebo effect (in which a patient feels better because he or she expects to feel better). Patients' expectations have been raised by the popular exorcism movement.
6. When *The Exorcist* was rereleased in 2000, the movie was again accompanied by a surge of interest in demonic possession and exorcism.

3. Examine the Author's Supporting Evidence

Michael W. Cuneo's article argues that the belief in demonic possession can be traced to cultural influences. To support these claims, he uses much the same kinds of evidence that M. Scott Peck uses—eyewitness testimony, statements of fact, and opinions and testimonials. He also relies on generalizations.

Eyewitness testimony (item 4). Unlike most skeptical arguments, Cuneo's article relies heavily on eyewitness testimony. While researching his book *American Exorcism* (2001), Cuneo, a sociologist, witnessed more than fifty exorcisms and did not see any demonic possession symptoms that he could not attribute to purely human causes.

Statements of fact (items 1 and 6). Cuneo claims that the idea of demonic possession caught on during the 1970s, a fact that would give credence to his argument that the novel and film *The Exorcist* can be credited with bringing it back into the public eye. He attempts to bolster this claim further by arguing that media interest in demonic possession noticeably increased following the rerelease of *The Exorcist* in 2000.

Opinions and testimonials (items 2–4, 6, and 8). Like many skeptical arguments, this piece relies heavily on opinions and testimonials. Cuneo includes many of his own professional judgments about the sociological movement surrounding possessions and exorcisms. He argues in item 2, for example, that the film *The Exorcist* played an important role in bringing ideas about possession and exorcism back into mainstream American culture. Similarly, he offers his professional testimony in item 4, stating that he has seen many exorcisms, none of which seemed to be an authentic case of demonic possession.

Generalizations (item 5). A generalization is a claim based on examples. For instance, an author might cite the cases of three people who like grapefruit juice, then generalize that everyone does. Although this sort of argument is sometimes classified as a fallacy, it is a necessary part of everyday reasoning. We can believe that gravity always works, or that people walk on their feet rather than on their hands, only by generalizing based on known cases. There are two types of generalizations:

1. *Explicit generalizations.* The author openly and directly argues that a generalization is true.

2. *Implied generalizations.* The author presents evidence that would logically lead the audience to generalize. For example, an author might describe three famous cases of dog attacks, leaving many readers with the impression that dogs are dangerous.

Item 5 is both eyewitness testimony and an explicit generalization. Based on his experience as a witness during fifty exorcisms, Cuneo extrapolates what he witnessed to other exorcisms (specifically stating that "this is how exorcisms tend to go").

4. Consider Alternative Hypotheses

Most proponents of exorcism believe that demons really possess human beings and cite the efficacy of exorcism as evidence that demonic possession is a real phenomenon. If the cure is spiritual, proponents suggest, then the disease is probably spiritual, too.

In considering this alternative hypothesis, Cuneo concedes that exorcism can be effective, but he argues that this is not because demonic possession is a real phenomenon. He attributes the success of exorcism primarily to the placebo effect (wherein a patient feels better because he or she expects to feel better), and he dismisses the idea that these patients were possessed by demons.

5. Draw Your Own Conclusion

You decide: Does Michael W. Cuneo make a good case that the belief in demonic possession can be attributed primarily to sociological factors? How would you rank it on our five-point scale?

Your Turn!

Choose one article from this book that has not already been analyzed and use hypothetical reasoning to decide whether the author's evidence supports the hypothesis. Here is a form you can use:

Name of article_____ Author_____

1. State the author's hypothesis.

2. Isolate the author's supporting evidence, listing each piece of evidence as part of a numbered list (as we did with the two articles analyzed above).

3. Examine the author's supporting evidence. Identify each type of evidence—is it eyewitness testimony, a statement of fact, a generalization, a personal opinion, a celebrity or expert testimonial, statistical evidence, ridicule, or something else entirely?

4. Consider alternative hypotheses. What alternative hypotheses does the author consider? Are they presented in a fair way? Can you think of any credible alternative hypotheses that the author might have missed?

5. Draw your own conclusion. Regardless of whether the author's hypothesis is true, does he or she make a good case for it?

William Alexander, *Demonic Possession in the New Testament.* Grand Rapids, MI: Baker Book House, 1980.

Thomas B. Allen, *Possessed: The True Story of an Exorcism.* New York: Doubleday, 1993.

Philip Almond, *Demonic Possession and Exorcism in Early Modern England.* New York: Cambridge University Press, 2004.

Gabriele Amorth, *An Exorcist: More Stories.* San Francisco: Ignatius, 2002.

———, *An Exorcist Tells His Story.* San Francisco: Ignatius, 1999.

Joe Beam, *Seeing the Unseen: Preparing Yourself for Spiritual Warfare.* West Monroe, LA: Howard, 2002.

Joel Bjorling, *Consulting Spirits: A Bibliography.* London: Greenwood, 1998.

Gerald Brittle, *The Demonologist: The Extraordinary Career of Ed and Lorraine Warren.* New York: St. Martin's, 1991.

Nancy Caciola, *Discerning Spirits: Divine and Demonic Possession in the Middle Ages.* New York: Cornell University Press, 2003.

Michael W. Cuneo, *American Exorcism: Expelling Demons in the Land of Plenty.* New York: Doubleday, 2001.

Winston Davis, *Dojo: Magic and Exorcism in Modern Japan.* Palo Alto, CA: Stanford University Press, 1982.

Graham Dwyer, *The Divine and the Demonic: Supernatural Affliction and Its Treatment in North India.* New York: Curzon/Routledge, 2003.

Martin Ebon, *The Devil's Bride: Exorcism Past and Present.* New York: Harper & Row, 1974.

——, *Exorcism: Fact Not Fiction.* New York: Signet, 1974.

Anthony Finlay, *Demons: The Devil, Possession, and Exorcism.* New York: Sterling, 2002.

Edith Fiore, *The Unquiet Dead: A Psychologist Treats Spirit Possession.* New York: Ballantine, 1991.

Felicitas D. Goodman, *The Exorcism of Anneliese Michel.* New York: Doubleday, 1981.

——, *How About Demons? Possession and Exorcism in the Modern World.* Bloomington: Indiana University Press, 1988.

Bruce Kapferer, *A Celebration of Demons: Exorcism and the Aesthetics of Healing in Sri Lanka.* New York: Smithsonian, 1991.

Bob Larson, *In the Name of Satan: How the Forces of Evil Work and What You Can Do to Defeat Them.* Nashville: Thomas Nelson, 1996.

——, *Larson's Book of Spiritual Warfare.* Nashville: Thomas Nelson, 1999.

Francis MacNutt, *Deliverance from Evil Spirits: A Practical Manual.* Grand Rapids, MI: Chosen Books, 1995.

Malachi Martin, *Hostage to the Devil: The Possession and Exorcism of Five Living Americans.* New York: Reader's Digest, 1976.

Traugott K. Oesterreich, *Possession and Exorcism: Among Primitive Races, in Antiquity, the Middle Ages, and Modern Times.* London: Kegal Paul, 1930.

Gaetano Paxia, *The Devil's Scourge: Exorcism During the Italian Renaissance*. York Beach, ME: Red Wheel/Weiser, 2002.

M. Scott Peck, *People of the Lie: The Hope for Healing Human Evil*. New York: Simon & Schuster, 1983.

Ralph Sarchie and Lisa Collier Cool, *Beware the Night: A New York City Cop Investigates the Supernatural*. New York: St. Martin's, 2001.

Margaret Thaler Singer and Janja Lalich, *"Crazy" Therapies: What Are They? Do They Work?* Hoboken, NJ: Jossey-Bass/Wiley, 1996.

Graham W. Twelftree, *Jesus the Exorcist: A Contribution to the Study of the Historical Jesus*. Philadephia: Coronet Books, 1993.

Ed Warren and Lorraine Warren, *Ghost Hunters: True Stories from the World's Most Famous Demonologists*. New York: St. Martin's, 1989.

———, *Werewolf: A True Story of Demonic Possession*. New York: St. Martin's, 1991.

Gershon Winkler, *Dybbuk: A Glimpse of the Supernatural in Jewish Tradition*. Brooklyn, NY: Judaica, 1981.

Friedrich Zuendel, *The Awakening: One Man's Battle with Darkness*. Robertsbridge, UK: Plough, 1999.

Index

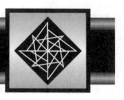